I0170949

The Discovery of Causeless Joy

How to be happy no matter what happens

Russel Brownlee

Copyright © 2015 by Russel Brownlee

Print Edition

ISBN: 978-0-620-64696-3

All rights reserved. This book or any portion thereof may not be reproduced or used in any manner whatsoever without the express written permission of the publisher except for the use of brief quotations in book reviews or articles.

Publisher: Russel Brownlee
Cape Town
South Africa
www.russelbrownlee.com

CONTENTS

FOREWORD

You know how you struggle to make yourself feel better or think positive or be a success – and it often just doesn't work? The more you try to rearrange your life so you can have things that bring you love, peace and joy – the more it seems you'll never get there.

What if I could tell you that there's a reason why you're not succeeding – and it has nothing to do with your abilities or your determination? And what if your failure to make things work for you is not because you're doing something wrong but because you're doing something right? You see, we've all been operating on a faulty premise – that what we seek is outside us and that we've got to do things to get other things that will bring us the inner qualities of joy and wellbeing that we long for. The world supports this perception – up to a point. And then it crashes.

Your inability to find what you are looking for is not because you're doing it wrong, it's because you are ready for the next stage of your evolution – the discovery that everything you seek is already within you. You can't get it right because you are already right. Your pain, your struggles and your failures say nothing about who you are, for you are that which is ever beyond failure or success, dark or light. Your pain does not need to be fixed or improved, it is simply a pointer to that which is beyond pain. Right now you are a perfect expression of the One, with all your faults still in place.

1

This book is an invitation to let go of the struggle of trying to fix and improve yourself and to discover the causeless joy of your true being. You can go on fixing and improving forever, or you can awaken to the perfection you already are. If you are a weary seeker, may this book bring the relief you are looking for.

1. INTRODUCTION

We all want to be happy.

In fact, for most of us the search for happiness is our main purpose in life. Whether we are looking for money, a career, a partner, children or any other material gain we are essentially looking for happiness. And if we are looking to change the world and make it a better place, we are still looking for happiness. Even the spiritual search – for God, enlightenment, inner peace – is a search for happiness.

We believe that one day, when certain conditions are met, we will be happy at last.

But how well is this working for us?

Sure, we feel happy some of the time – usually when we get something we've been wanting or we reach a place in our lives where our needs are being met. And then, after a little while, something changes and our little bit of heaven begins to fade. Pretty soon we're on the treadmill again, trying to organise life to bring us what we want and need.

Almost every institution of authority on our planet tells us that our purpose is to succeed by having more and getting what we want. Religions tell us that if we follow certain rules and cut out certain behaviours, we will be saved – one day. Schools and universities tell us that if we study hard and get the right education, we will get good jobs and be productive members of society and, one day, we will be happy. Our social traditions tell us that if we just find the right man or woman and settle down with them and bring up healthy children in a loving environment we will be happy. Oh, and we should also have one or two cars in the garage and a really good medical plan. And let's not even turn on the television because every commercial will tell us about something we really need if we want to finally make it and be happy.

And what about our psychologies and self-help philosophies – don't these help us get what we really, really want? Well, some might – but a lot of them are also about all the things you've got to do to be a fully functional, productive member of society. If you just do this and avoid that, you'll be fine. First you've got to sort out your childhood issues and your mother/father issues and your money issues and your fear of commitment and your addictions and that thing you do where you use cream puffs and doughnuts as a substitute for real love. In other words, if you just get it right – then you'll be happy.

And once again, your happiness is deferred.

If you've been on this trip for a number of years you might have had some highs but you will probably also have hit some real lows. In fact, doesn't the thought of having to go through one more course of therapy or do one more workshop make you feel a little ill? *When, oh when, will I finally get it right and be happy? What's wrong with me?*

Perhaps you are in this place right now. If so, you might find this book quite refreshing. You see, there is a place for fixing ourselves and doing our therapy and working on our relationships and clearing our money issues. But at a certain point you might get the suspicion that you can go on fixing and improving forever and the work will never be done, and you still won't be happy. This moment can be one of deep and prolonged crisis, perhaps even deepening into the mystical process known as the Dark Night of the Soul. But what awaits on the other side is a new world and a whole new model of existence. I want to introduce you to this new way so that your endless searching might at last come to rest and you might find the happiness, joy and wellbeing that is already within you.

You see, in the end we really can go on fixing and improving forever, and all we will have is a nicely polished, highly functional ego. A wonder to behold, but still limited, still searching for peace and love. You know already that the ego cannot give you what you really want. But perhaps you don't know how to go beyond the ego to what is already here, utterly untouched by all your faults, weaknesses, strengths and other accoutrements of the separate self. You are already the joy that you seek. All it requires is that you stop and notice it.

Easier said than done, however, and that's why you're holding a whole book and not just a single page or a single line.

Neither shall they say, 'See here!' or, 'See there!' for, behold, the Kingdom of God is within you. (Luke 17:21)

That's really the whole of it and we could end right here. But let's stretch it out a bit and take our time.

My story

When I was young I felt that I had some important contribution to give to the world. I was full of ambition to give this gift, whatever it was. And so I pursued various careers. Because I was good at writing I thought I would be a journalist and change the world through courageous reporting and moving tales of injustice and struggle. On my first day on my very first job as a journalist my manager took one look at me and said, "Russel, you're too introverted to be a journalist. You're not going to make it." Needless to say, I was quite indignant and I assured him he was wrong. Four years later I knew he was right and I left journalism and undertook some aimless wanderings. I felt the call to write a novel, and this was taking up all my time and energy. I thought that if I wrote a book that moved people and answered some of life's deeper questions, I would find my place in the world. I would be an author. It took four years to write that book, and when it was finished I knew it was not very good, so I started another. I was working as a text editor at this time – not a glamorous job or well paid, but it gave me the time to write. Book number 2 was barely an improvement on the first, and so I began book number 3. This one was different and was published and found some critical approval. Finally I had arrived.

Or had I? Now the reality sunk in. I was just about penniless, and though I was published the royalties were little more than pocket money. I simply did not have the resources to continue writing. And worse, when I picked up my pen to begin another book, I found myself writing five or six different stories, none of which had any power or impetus. The situation continued for years and I felt a great sense of loss. My writing had abandoned me, and I had no career to speak of. I began training in therapy and coaching, but while my introverted, introspective nature made me good at this work, it also made me lousy at selling my services. The result was that at the age of around 48, when most of my peers were well settled, I was living month to month, constantly harassed by the need to earn money in ways that felt burdensome to me. I wondered what had happened to that bright, shiny thing I had come to give the world, and why I was getting it all so wrong, and why the spiritual light that had fired me up when I was just a boy had dimmed to nothing.

Somewhere in those years of adulthood a blinding insight had come to me, that God did not exist, and neither did I. If God was a concept, then so was I. When I spoke of this to people they thought I was being weird. I read of some people who had had similar insights, but theirs had resulted in enlightenment, while mine had stripped me of my will and purpose. Whenever I did anything a voice inside me would ask, "Who?" Who is doing this? Who is deciding this? While other people were happily saying things like, "I'm just going down to the shops to buy some bread," the voice inside me would ask, "Who?" Who is this one who decides to do anything? When I looked for that one I could find nothing. When God vanished, I vanished, and yet whatever remained was weighed down with almost constant pain. I could not believe there was anybody in here to do anything, and yet still I cast around, looking for the right thing to do. For years I felt I was being cooked, boiled, rendered down to nothing. Meditation brought some relief, but I was no longer looking for light or inner presence for I knew that anything that presented itself as something other than me, as an object, would be illusion. I simply sat and boiled. And while I did this I slid into the heaviness of something near depression. Whatever I did to shift it or to bring in light would only make it worse. I dreamt of suicide, but once again that voice arose, "Who?" Who would kill whom? Quite clearly there were two of us in here, one of whom spoke and the other who was ever silent. All this time I was trying to write another novel. Not surprisingly, none of it went anywhere.

So now you are probably wondering what happened next. I wish I could tell you I had some kind of revelation, but I didn't. Instead, on some very dark day when I could see no light at all, I became aware of something I can only call faith. Not faith in some God, but faith in the bare fact of existence. I realised that even in this pain, the light was on. Something of the miracle of ordinary awareness shone through and I realised that in all the disappointment and confusion of my life, there had been this constant alive, awakeness. This bare, undeniable fact of pure existence struck me as something worth having faith in. I glimpsed in that pure existence a stillness and love that was ancient, vast, subtle ... so still that I had overlooked it again and again. This stillness and peace was present even though my dominant sense was one of pain. This was the real revelation – that it was possible to be in touch with peace while at the same time experiencing painful thoughts about life circumstances. The peace seemed to come from an entirely different order of existence that was untouched by whatever I was experiencing. This realisation did not catapult me out of my distress for it was too tenuous and fragile. But it did answer the question of who was doing everything. The "who" was this stillness, this transpersonal space which I experienced as peace and subtle joy. I, this separate self, was only appearing to do anything. I wish I could say that this revelation was an event that transformed my vision forever, but the truth is that it is something that I have to work at through moment to moment practices, which I will outline in this book. I have found that those teachers who fall into enlightenment in a sudden event are often very inspiring in their writings but are not very helpful for those of us taking the scenic route. This book is for the majority of people who unpack the secrets of their true nature over time, undergoing the trials and joys of a slow awakening.

If this describes you, then welcome. My hope is that these words point you to the greatness that you already are, despite all the imperfections that seem to confirm your lack and unworthiness. The good news is that you already are all that you seek, and nothing that you experience in this world says anything about who you really are. Our work is not to fix everything and get it right, it's to see that we are already right, no matter what is happening.

A few words on God

I use the God word quite liberally throughout this book, so I feel it necessary to clarify my use of it. When I set out on my spiritual journey a long time ago I thought of God as some kind of supreme being. I felt a strong sense of devotion to this being and I desired to be closer to it. Over the years the devotion has remained but the God-concept has changed. If I believe that God is ultimate love, then it makes no sense that He, She, It, should be separate from me, for separation is the denial of love. Therefore the God whom I seek is none other than my own Self, and the one who seeks this God is none other than God itself.

That said, I often use the God word in the old-fashioned sense to refer to the God idea in us which we have picked up through religious education or simply through absorbing the language forms of our society. We have a natural tendency to project our qualities onto others, and the ultimate projection is the God/Satan projection. All our good qualities go to one of them and our bad qualities go to the other. The God concept is hardwired into us and is kept in place by language. Our minds and our language can only deal in concepts and in things that are distinct from other things, so when we perceive a loving presence that seems to come from outside our individual consciousness we assume it must be some kind of Other. Sometimes we call it God. Or sometimes we deny it completely. My contention is that the feeling of the presence of God, in other words, the presence of some benevolent Other, is in fact the experience of pure awareness becoming aware of itself. Awareness, it turns out, can be aware of awareness. This phenomenon gives the appearance of a subject being loved unconditionally by an object, but it is really the One gazing upon itself and discovering that it is love.

Sometimes when I use the God word I am referring to this love relationship of the Self for the Self. You might prefer to use different words. "Life" will work just as well. And for those of a more scientific persuasion, you could consider the term "implicate order". Everything that is said about the implicate order is true of the realm of God. No time, no space, etcetera. What the purely scientific view lacks, however, is allowance for the phenomenon of Presence, which is the awareness of awareness. The felt experience of the implicate order is not one of empty, subatomic space, it is one of aware substance, a felt presence of Being. What the mystics have called the Presence of God is simply this Presence or self-aware, non-personal intelligence.

Much of what I have just said has been an attempt to reassure any avowed atheists reading this that they are not required to give up their faith. However, for them I also have a little challenge: Do you think that by eliminating the belief in God you have really set yourself free of concepts that tie you down? God is just one of many projections. The most profound and most limiting is the projection of a self, an ego. If you believe you are a "me" acting in the world then you are still infected with the God concept, though you choose to call it by another name. Sometimes when I use the God word I am referring to the god of the little self, the god that some atheists worship.

One of the ironies of the spiritual path is that those who are truly awakened are the only ones who really have no God-concept. Not only have they discarded the bearded deity in the sky, they have discarded all belief in a separate self who acts independently of the world. They have found the utter emptiness that is also the utter fullness of existence. This book will point to how we might begin to live from this awareness right now.

So, atheists, theists, ragged pilgrims, god-drunk lovers, let us continue.

2. CRACKS IN THE SYSTEM

A paradigm is a model of perception or way of interpreting and describing an aspect of reality. For example, the Newtonian model of science is a paradigm. It interprets the physical universe through the lens of force, motion and distance. For a long time it was assumed that this paradigm would hold true for the whole universe, but then someone discovered quantum physics, and a new scientific paradigm was born.

Our view of ourselves as individuals with needs that must be fulfilled is often taken as the truth of who we are, but it is really just a model, a paradigm. Paradigms give us handy ways of describing and understanding reality, but ultimately they are all merely models and not the whole truth. In this chapter I will outline some of the myths and illusions that expose the weak points in our current self-development paradigm. By doing this, I hope to show you how some of your apparent failures have not been because you have been doing things wrong but because you have come up against the limits of the model you are trying to work within. When you can see why things aren't working, you can be receptive to a new paradigm that accommodates a more expanded view of reality.

The Myth of Progress

Our current self-development paradigm holds that we are born with faults and have to overcome those faults in order to be better people. Some of us are born with an internal sense of what is right and wrong, but even then we have to work on ourselves to achieve happiness and fulfilment. We believe that we have to overcome our pettiness and our jealousy and our anger if we are to become spiritually mature. And we have to achieve certain things, like a quiet mind and a full bank account.

This self-development paradigm views life as a school in which we start off not knowing much and then we work hard, pass tests, gather achievements and eventually graduate. After that, we continue getting better and better as we improve ourselves more and more. The assumption of this model is that if we improve ourselves and fix our issues we will eventually graduate and attain what we desire. It's a model based on the school system, and like all good models it works, until the point when it doesn't.

For many of us, the spiritual quest is also informed by this paradigm of incremental progress, ending in enlightenment or union with God or some kind of blissful happiness. We pray, we meditate, we go on courses and we read books that show us how to improve ourselves and eventually attain our spiritual goal. It is hoped that through diligent labour we will make progress and eventually enjoy success.

But here's the problem – while the paradigm of self-improvement might hold true for the development of the ego, it does not hold true for the development of the spirit. In fact, the spirit cannot develop because it is already all it will ever be. The paradigm of spiritual progress says we will get to enlightenment or freedom or happiness through constant improvement, but this model has failure built right into it. You cannot achieve what you already are. In fact, the more you try to get it, the more you distract yourself from seeing what is already here. I unpack this idea through the rest of the book, but for now just consider that the model of progress works for the physical and psychological aspects of your life, but not the truly spiritual. And by spiritual I mean that aspect of consciousness that is already whole and complete and never in need of improvement.

The Great Reversal

What do we feel we really know about ourselves and the world?

Well, it seems common knowledge that there is a world out there and we are in here, acting on the world. Most evidence seems to point in this direction. When I use will and intention and I act on the world, things go better than when I just lie around doing nothing. I have the power to change my circumstances. When I decide something inside and act on the world outside, I often get the results I expect. From this I conclude that what I seek is truly outside of me.

After all, everything I have learnt from my schooling to my cultural conditioning tells me that if I do certain things I will get certain other things, and this will contribute to my wellbeing and make me feel good. If I get a job, I will be happy. If I get a loving partner, I will be happy. If I pray or meditate in the right way, I will receive the rewards of my efforts and I will be happy.

If we reduce all this to the underlying paradigm, it can be expressed as the belief that what we seek is outside of us. The money, the lifestyle, the partner, the deity, the nirvana, the heaven ... it's all some kind of state or condition that we must attain because right now we are separate from it.

I call this the outside-in model of the universe. Like all successful models, it works – up to a point.

The specific point at which this model begins to show signs of fatigue is towards the end of what I call the Empowerment stage (more on this later). All this achieving of things in the outer world and all this following of the rules for success and happiness – and still we're not happy! What's wrong with us?

Well, of course, nothing. We're simply discovering the limits of one paradigm and opening to another. The new paradigm is 180 degrees in the opposite direction to the old one. I call the new paradigm the inside-out model. In this model, we understand that everything we seek is already within us. Our work is to find it within and then express it outwardly. By contrast, in the outside-in model, we look outside for the good things so we can feel good inside.

In the new model we are finding the good inside and then expressing this pre-existing goodness in the outer world. Author and spiritual teacher Derek Rydall calls this inside-out approach the Law of Emergence. Our goodness emerges from within ourselves, just as the oak emerges from the acorn. The acorn doesn't have to go looking for the oak tree – it just has to surrender to the oak tree already within it. Derek has a great term for the 180 degree turnaround that I am describing here – the Great Reversal.

The Great Reversal is the belief that what you seek is outside you and needs to be found. It is exactly opposite to how things really are. Sure, you can get quite far on the belief that your good is outside you and somewhere off in the future, but at some point the cracks are going to show and you'll be ready for the next stage. When that happens, you experience the Big Betrayal (another term I'm borrowing from Derek).

The Big Betrayal

The Big Betrayal is the moment when the cracks caused by the Great Reversal get so huge that the system collapses. For example, you might experience a business loss despite doing all the right things and being positive and using the Law of

Attraction. Or you get ill, despite thinking only wholesome thoughts and eating organic and doing all sorts of therapies to release your repressed anger. The Big Betrayal is the moment when the world betrays your efforts to locate your success in the outside world. It feels traumatic, but it's actually a merciful event because it begins the correction of the Great Reversal. Once you've processed the Big Betrayal (and there might be many!) you begin to see things from the new inside-out paradigm, finding your good within you and in the present moment, rather than outside and in the past or future. The Big Betrayal can be part of the Dark Night of the Soul, the mystical process in which your previous understanding is stripped away so that something new might be revealed.

In the old paradigm you are looking for God, the good, outside of you in a set of conditions you believe must be met. This includes trying to attain certain so-called spiritual conditions and states. When you experience happiness it is because something desirable has happened or something undesirable has stopped. The conditions for your happiness have been met. In this scenario, your joy is dependent on conditions, on causes. As long as you believe you need a cause for joy, you will always be on the go, trying to manipulate reality to bring you the conditions you believe necessary for your fulfilment. And where does this all end up? In the Big Betrayal. Life will find ways to wake you up from your illusion. Only when you let go of causes and conditions will you be open to the joy that is already here for you, utterly without cause. Your true nature is joy, peace, power, wellbeing. The oak of your fully enlightened self is already within the acorn of your present appearance. You don't need to find enlightenment or happiness, it is already here. If you try to meddle with the system and attempt to be the best and shiniest acorn in the forest you will never discover the greatness that is within you. For the oak to be born, the acorn must die. This is why it sometimes feels painful – your acorn existence is proving too small for the greatness that is emerging through you and as you. Surrender to the dissolution of your acorn self, even though you cannot yet see what awaits you. The acorn can never imagine the oak. The caterpillar cannot imagine the butterfly. The idea here is to let go of intending how things should turn out and surrender to the unimaginable that is already taking shape in you.

The Feeling Fallacy

In the conventional view of reality, we feel bad because something bad is happening in the world and we feel good because something good is happening. For instance, if we lose our job we feel bad because now, well, we're unemployed and suddenly have no income. If a month or two later we find a new, better job, we are happy again. The bad thing turned out to be a good thing.

In this view of life, we spend our time trying to make good things happen so we can feel good, while avoiding bad things that make us feel bad. The vast majority of the world's population is engaged in this endeavour, earnestly trying to change reality so that they can finally feel good. While this tactic works some of the time, it also ties us to a cycle of doing, striving and efforting that ultimately fails to deliver on the freedom it promises.

Here's what we're not getting. The world itself is neutral and simply exists as a series of facts. It is people who attach a story to what those facts mean. "I lost my job and now I don't know what to do," is a story. The facts are much simpler: "I am not required to go to the office tomorrow."

We assume that God or some other authority has declared the meanings of things and that if we don't ascribe to these meanings we're doing something wrong. Losing a job is bad, being assaulted is bad, being abused is bad. But these are all stories that we attach to situations based on our interpretations of what is happening and on our belief systems. Reality itself is just a series of events with no story.

Why am I going on about this?

Well, if reality is neutral, then our feelings about what happens come not from the world but from our thoughts about what is happening. If we feel bad, the bad feeling is telling us about our thoughts – not about the world. As author/coach Michael Neill says, we live in the feeling of our thoughts, not in the feeling of the world.

Maybe take a moment to really let this sink in: Your feelings are telling you about your thoughts, not about the world.

In this understanding, good feelings indicate that your thoughts are aligned with the truth of who you are and bad feelings indicate that your thoughts are out of alignment with the truth of your inner being. The badness is not out there in the world, it's within you. Your feelings are an emotional guidance system that accurately tell you whether your thinking is aligned with how things are or whether they are arising from a faulty interpretation.

So if you are feeling upset over losing a job, the upset is not saying that the event of losing your job is bad or that you have failed (it is impossible for you to fail) – it's saying that your interpretation of it as a loss and as something that shouldn't be happening is inaccurate. Your emotional guidance system is giving you immediate feedback on your interpretation so that you can step away from that story and allow a more truthful one to appear.

This insight can be liberating. It can also be quite challenging. Do you feel bad about abuse and cruelty? What about terrorists who cut off people's heads with kitchen knives? Our pain and revulsion is a reaction to the judgement within ourselves that these things are inherently bad. Because in this reality, nothing is inherently good or bad. Good and bad are stories that we tell. Life is trying to wake us up from the dream of interpretation. In this moment, right now, in the light of pure awareness, things are just happening and any story that appears is just one more happening.

This is why the conventional approach that tries to arrange things in the outer world to give you only good feelings will always fail you. It will fail because it is based on the fallacy that your feelings tell you the truth about the world. Your feelings tell you about your state of alignment with the truth of unconditional love. If you see loss, your interpretation of this as bad and unwanted will generate a discordant feeling in you. God has no opinion on your apparent loss, for in unity consciousness loss and gain are not possible. Loss is simply a dream. Your bad feeling is telling you that how you are thinking is discordant with how God or Reality is thinking.

We assume that God has declared some things good and some bad. If you don't have a conscious belief in God, then tune in to that part of you that assumes the good and bad of various situations. For instance, is it bad that children go hungry and sleep on the streets? Most of us will say yes, and then we suffer when we see this happening. We assume there is a right and wrong inherent in the world, or some state of rightness to which we should aspire. That is why our theologies cannot cope with events like the Holocaust. Where was God at Auschwitz? We assume God has an opinion and is separate from people and events. The only way to answer the "Where was God?" question is to see God in everything, the good and the bad. And yes, that does mean in the Nazis. God is the victim and the oppressor. God is as much the Nazi as any saint who has walked the earth. God is what is. God/Life

18

is calling to us to go beyond the good and bad and discover the consciousness that contains everything.

This is a huge understanding – too huge for the mind to comprehend. Simply feel into it and see if it resonates with you, even if it feels too "out there" or beyond the scope of your being to allow. I am not saying that I have reached a place of acceptance with the apparent bad things that happen, and I don't have to. All I need to be able to do is look to my thoughts when I feel bad rather than to pass judgement on the world. I need to see the monsters in me, first, before I see them out there. It is a practice of deep compassion and courage. One doesn't have to love the monsters, one only has to love oneself as one suffers under the illusion that there are monsters and that God, the good, is absent. It's not about changing the world to put more of God in it, it's about seeing God in everything, even in our own pain, revulsion and non-acceptance.

Your pain is not because of something that is happening to you, it is your God-self telling you that your interpretation of events is godless. It is an invitation to look again at events and to simply drop all interpretations. If you put a better-feeling story in place, that's a partial solution, because you're still attached to a story. Simply stop, notice your feelings and allow them. The allowing is coming from a place beyond good and evil - from your Buddha-nature or Christ consciousness. From this place a new perception will flow that brings more light and ease.

But get this – your pain might still remain. If you see cruelty in the world, the physical body will be alarmed and your strong desire for love and peace will be triggered. We must be compassionate with ourselves and not expect things to suddenly feel all groovy simply because we now have a new understanding of where our bad feelings come from. We are human and will suffer under our human interpretations. Our bodies will experience pain. Our minds will continue to misinterpret reality because they simply cannot grasp something that is boundless. What is left, then, is to allow the pain that comes from our humanness and our existence as creatures of duality.

While your divine nature is ever beyond suffering, your human nature will inevitably suffer. However, when you know that your bad feelings are not because of badness in the world, you might find yourself more able to surrender to what is. You might hold your life more lightly. You might let slights and attacks go more easily. Even though you might pray for this cup to pass you by, and it doesn't, you might find you have access to the grace that makes it bearable, even beautiful.

The Lie of Attraction

The Law of Attraction is a principle of the universe which says that similar things are attracted to one another. Positive thoughts attract more positive thoughts and therefore more opportunities, and negative thoughts attract more negativity and close down our receptivity to opportunity. So far so good. The problem comes in when we use the Law of Attraction as a strategy for creating happiness. I call this the Lie of Attraction. The Lie of Attraction is the belief that the Law of Attraction will bring us what we are really looking for. You see, if you imagine yourself as a little you over here who is trying to get stuff over there, you are reinforcing your separateness from life and all that is. You are affirming the duality that will continue to thwart your deeper desire for union and true bliss.

The Lie of Attraction is part of the existing paradigm – what I call the outside-in model. It says that your good is outside you somewhere and you must do certain things, like thinking positively and using intention, in order to attract good things to you. It's really all about me, me, me. Which all works very well, up to a point. That point is where you realise that whatever you create through the outside-in model will only bring you relative pleasures, it will not bring you the freedom from circumstance and effort that you truly seek.

As you will see in the next chapter, using the Law of Attraction to create desired outcomes is an activity of Empowerment consciousness. There's nothing wrong with this at all and working with the Law of Attraction can be of great benefit. It's just that many people who work with attraction-based techniques tend to forget about the Big Betrayal – the tendency of Life to eventually betray all outside-in constructions. If your enlightenment or joy depends on happy feelings and circumstances of any kind, Life will find a way to direct your attention into the realm of causeless perfection that is the real goal of your quest. If you are longing for true liberation then you will want to go deeper than the standard Empowerment practices that are so popular now. And that's just what we're doing in this book.

The Happiness Trap

Many years ago the Buddha discovered the secret of happiness. As an earnest seeker of truth he had spent the best part of his life pursuing the good of spiritual advancement and trying to master (avoid) the negativity and suffering that always seemed to be with him. Eventually, in a state of utter disillusionment, he sat down under a tree and declared he would not get up until he was enlightened.

Did he suddenly fall into bliss at that moment? No, in fact every demon in the universe came to him and tempted and taunted him. In modern language we would say that all his negativity and his wayward thoughts and his guilt and fear overwhelmed him. Once he stopped running from this stuff and trying to meditate it away, there it all was, just waiting for him to experience it. Well, Siddhartha sat and experienced it all, and then at a certain point the realisation hit him: No matter how much work he did and how many austerities he performed he would never get rid of these pesky demons. He saw that suffering, or rather the unsatisfactoriness of life, would always be with us. There would always be angels and demons and no amount of praying would swing the balance completely in one of their directions. He observed that the way he and most of the world were trying to find happiness (or enlightenment) was to chase after the good things and avoid the bad things. But now here he was, an expert chaser and avoider, finally facing the fact that the demons of his lower nature were as strong as when he first set out on the path. And that became his enlightenment. He declared that enlightenment was right here, right now, in the midst of all that was happening. The secret to happiness was not to keep chasing after the good and avoiding the bad because these dualities would always be with us. The position of true peace was in recognising all events and circumstances, including experiences of happiness and pain, as mere objects of awareness. We are not meant to try and change everything to get a feeling of peace (the outside-in model) but rather to discover the peace that is already our true nature.

Well, 2 400 years later and most of us are still chasing after the good stuff and avoiding the bad stuff and hoping we'll beat the unsatisfactoriness of life. We are happy when we win and sad when we lose. We persist in our ignorance, hoping that one day we will finally get it right and have everything in our lives nicely arranged so that we are no longer beset by our darker emotions and experiences. But how well is this working for us?

Contemporary teacher Kåre Landfald comments that the main cause of our suffering is our avoidance of suffering. If we just accept that suffering exists and that the dualistic nature of this reality will always bring us ups and downs, we can relax into the flow of life as it is, not feeling compelled to avoid negatives or chase after positives. This does not mean that we sit and do nothing all the time, it simply means that we release our cravings and aversions. It means we go out and do fun stuff and pursue the good things in life, but that we do not attach to those possessions and experiences. At some point the tide will turn and we will experience the shadow side of things. When that happens, we know it is not because we are doing it wrong, it's simply because life is bringing the next experience.

Peace begins when we stop trying to avoid our negativity but open to experiencing it. This does not mean we stay in a bad relationship or refuse to move from an unhealthy physical situation, it is simply that we stop fighting with our inner experience of these circumstances. If we are feeling pain, we acknowledge it, feel it, and open to what wants to happen next. Maybe it will be to take some kind of action. Maybe it will be to sit still. When we are not trying to avoid it we open to the actions and attitudes that want to arise from our already-present wholeness. These attitudes and actions do not bring us wholeness, they are reflections and enactments of the wholeness that already exists. We will tell a story of how they have brought us beneficial results, but really the result is already achieved when we cease resisting and open to the flow of wholeness into our situation.

The key quality we need to cultivate here is the ability to tolerate discomfort. If we know that discomfort is a part of the natural flow of experience, we no longer need to invest so much time in avoiding it. We can simply be with it and work with it. When discomfort arises, that is an appearance of the Now and is already deeply accepted by Life.

Our desire to avoid discomfort and experience only good feelings is what I call the Happiness Trap. We are taught that getting things to go our way is what we have to do if we want to survive and thrive. There is some truth in it, but it has become clouded by what is not true. The truth is that if you are in danger or if something is not in your highest interest, you are called to get the hell out of there. That is not avoidance – it is right action. This is the key distinction. Our avoidance of pain and discomfort means we are closed to the flow of right action that arises from our deeper intelligence. Only by accepting and allowing the pain can we open to the best thing to do about it. If we view it as bad and complain about it, we are in aversion and have blocked our connection with right action. But if we say, "OK, I'm feeling triggered right now, let's just be with this for a moment and see what's really going on," then we have demonstrated non-attachment to the condition and it is free to move.

What keeps suffering locked in place is our belief that we shouldn't be suffering. Unwittingly, we have attached to an outcome of feeling good, when the Now is the truth of the experience of suffering. The technique here is simple. Stop, notice the pain and your resistance, and allow both to be there. In this allowing, you step into the space beyond outcomes where you can experience whatever discomfort or challenge is arising in a free and open way. This freedom of non-avoidance and non-craving is the medicine that will bring ease and right-action into the situation.

The Buddha tells us life will have its ups and downs. That's the bad news. The good news is that there is nothing we have to do to try and make everything straight. Allow the ups and downs and cease with thinking we have to change reality in order to be happy. Happiness comes from making peace with the up and down of things and discovering our true nature as that which is ever beyond ups and downs.

The Myth of the Self

The final illusion is the illusion of the separate self. This is perhaps the most difficult to understand, but it is the key to all the other illusions. Our conventional models of spiritual and self-development hold that we are individuals with separate selves. The separate self is seen externally in the form of separate bodies, and internally it is a felt sense of individuality. In spiritual terms, we are believed to have souls that learn, grow and achieve – moving ever closer to God or enlightenment. The feeling of separation is strengthened by our history and our memories. Clearly, my life experiences are different to yours, so we are separate beings.

In this model, our work as spiritually mature individuals is to overcome our weaknesses, heal our hurts, be nice, and achieve happiness through getting our needs met. We feel we have a life, a destiny, a path. When we look inside, we feel genuinely individual. When we speak, we use the words "I" and "me" and it really feels that these terms relate to a real person inside us who is, well, us.

And so we set out into the world to learn, do and achieve. We make the most of our lives and hope to accumulate what is needed to create happiness. At some stage we probably embark on a spiritual quest, and even this is perceived as an individual journey of a self towards some spiritual object.

In short, the self is always maintained. The self is ever a subject, seeking an object. And how well is this working for us? No matter how often we fail, we persist with the notion that if we just have some more time and more knowledge and better circumstances, we will find what we are looking for. The subject, I, will be united with the object of its desire. In that moment, so the fantasy goes, the self will be exalted and will have finally achieved what it set out to achieve.

Except for one small problem. Quite logically, if I am seeking union with all that is, I will not be around when that union happens. The individual I is separate from the all and so cannot survive the moment of union. For union to happen, the I must die.

When we perform practices, do affirmations and strive to be good, we are affirming an I who is doing all this, and with that we push the object of our desire ever further from our reach. It is like a donkey chasing after the carrot dangling from a stick above its head. No matter how hard you try to reach heaven or your final reward, the you who desires it can never reach it. This is the paradox of enlightenment.

Underneath all your desire for a loving partner, for health, for wealth, is a desire for union with God, all that is. It is a desire for the cessation of the separate self and the resurrection as the One self. You might not have put it in those words, but underneath all your quests is this calling to the deep rest and peace of oneness. We would all be there right now if not for the persistent and convincing belief that we are individuals on a path to perfection.

The separate self is a useful vehicle for exploring the creation. For a while it busies itself with creating things and perfecting the world and itself. But then it discovers that no matter what it does, it is still separate, still alone. At that point it begins to be plagued by a great doubt. What if I do not exist? Or what if this being I take myself to be is not as solid and well-defined as I had thought? At this point the notion of a separate self who is master of his destiny begins to crumble. What is revealed is that the separate self is really just a belief, a model. It works a lot of the time, but when stressed it starts to show its flaws.

This short chapter is not adequate to fully go into this subject, so all I am doing here is inviting you to question the basic assumption of your separateness. We don't have to suddenly step into full unity consciousness to benefit from what is being outlined in this book. It is enough that we pause and consider the evidence before us, and then move forward with a sense of openness to something new. By the end of the book I hope to have given you a taste of unity consciousness, and you will have seen how it is not as threatening or as "out there" as the mind will let you believe. The I is surrendered very gracefully and is reborn as Presence. When you use the word "I" from a state of Presence you are referring to something that is far greater than the small you who has a name and lives at a certain address. You are still there, and yet you are not the you that you were before.

I was wondering how to put this concept of no-self into more of a concrete example when I began to pay attention to how I was feeling right in that moment. I had just written this chapter and was beginning to feel some doubt as to whether it belonged in this book, whether it was too theoretical, or whether my intended reader would think it a bit too way out. In short, I became beset by doubts. The doubts began to extend to the rest of the book and I wondered who I was to think that I could write about the myth of the self or causeless joy, or in fact anything at all. However, in catching myself doing this I realised that such thoughts were typical of the small I, the ego self. If ego comprises my whole world, then I will categorise my endeavours in terms of success or failure, good or bad. So on some days I will think I am writing like an angel, and on other days I will think I should just give up and get a day job. This type of black and white thinking is typical of the egoic self.

So, having realised that I was getting trapped in duality, I simply noticed what was happening without trying to shift anything or to think differently. I just noticed that certain interpretations were happening, and I opened to the possibility that other interpretations might also be valid. In that moment the insight came to me that it was not entirely true to say that I had written this chapter. Sure, if a video had been running it would have shown me sitting here writing, but did that mean that I, little old me, was actually the cause of this writing? I didn't have an answer, but something opened up in my awareness. It was more like the writing of this chapter had happened, and I was along for the ride. In the light of this perception, it made no sense to think about whether the message would be received or not, or whether the writing was any good. The writing was just what it was – neither good nor bad. In one sense I had written it, but in another sense I had not. The writing was its own thing, and I didn't have to worry about how it would be received. All I had to do was show up at the page and surrender to what wanted to happen.

Imagine now if you could live all your life from this perception. The self appears, and yet it is fluid and light. It does not attach to outcomes. You have a sense both of living your life and of being lived by life. You are at once an individual and at once beyond all individuality. But do not think about this, just feel it and know it. You did not make yourself read these words; reading just happened. Your reactions to these words also did not arise through any action on your behalf; they simply appeared. Your liking or disliking, your recognition or your rejection ... were you actually involved in any of this? Or did thoughts and sensations simply appear?

Notice how often in the course of a day you are not at all aware of yourself, and yet thoughts, perceptions and sensations continue to arise. Might it be at least partly true that you are not living your life but that life is living through you and as you?

And whatever you answered, just notice where that answer came from.

Did you really think it, or did it just appear?

3. A NEW PARADIGM

In the previous chapter I outlined our existing, outside-in model for understanding our lives and I identified some of its limitations. My main aim here was to help you understand why your efforts to change reality and to succeed might not all be working as well as you expected them to. The reason is not that you are failing to grasp how the model works, it is that you have reached the limits of the model and are ready for something new.

To really understand the new paradigm and how it differs from the old one, we need to take a look at the broad stages of consciousness development that individuals and cultures pass through as they evolve. This will give us a map of the territory so we no longer have to spend too much time on paths that don't get us where we really want to go.

Four stages of spiritual development

Once upon a time there was a prince who had to go into battle against some of his relatives who had allied themselves with an evil king. As the prince stood in his chariot waiting to go into battle he was overcome with a great inner conflict. If he fought, he would be responsible for the death of relatives and former friends. But if he turned away from the battle, he would allow evil to triumph. In the grip of this dilemma, he prayed for help, and at that moment a divine being appeared before him. This being informed the prince that his torment was because of a fundamental misunderstanding of reality. He was taking himself to be the doer of his actions, whereas in fact he was not. The actions were happening by themselves as a result of the moods of nature. The divine being's message to the prince was that he should do what he had to do without attachment to the outcome. If he ended up killing relatives in a battle he could not escape, that was the divine order of things and it wasn't up to him to try and arrange things to his liking. The true purpose of the warrior was to fight without thought for gain or loss, and in so doing he would transcend his lower self and attain the perspective of the gods.

Some of you will have recognised this as the story of Arjuna and Krishna from the Bhagavad Gita, a book of Hindu scripture written more than 2 000 years ago.

The god Krishna tells Arjuna that he will not solve his conflict by trying to choose one option that is better than another. The divine perspective is the third position from which all options are seen as equal expressions of oneness. Krishna says that all actions and events arise not from the will of people but from the moods of nature. In the scriptures these moods are called the three gunas. The gunas are tamas, rajas and sattva.

Tamas is the energy of sloth, lethargy, confusion and ignorance.

Rajas is the energy of action, vitality, progress, invention and restlessness.

Sattva is the energy of purity, completion, truth and rest.

These moods express themselves in the activities and preferences of our daily lives. One might find oneself gravitating more to one of them than the other, or perhaps there are parts of one's life where tamas predominates, and other parts where rajas is active. Let's see how these energies relate to something simple like our food:

- Tamasic food: Fast foods, high sugar and fat, emotional eating, fast-food chains (emphasis on convenience and mood-enhancement)

- Rajasic food: Cuisine, fine dining, MasterChef, diet plans, upmarket restaurants, cooking competitions, glossy cooking books (emphasis on technique and achievement)

- Sattvic food: Simple, mostly vegetarian, wholesome, nourishing, simple flavours, (made with love and awareness)

While you might never have heard of the three gunas, you will probably be able to relate to them more when we see them as the motivating tendencies behind the three broad stages of spiritual development, namely Victimhood, Empowerment and Wisdom (sometimes also called Surrender).

Tamas is the stage of victimhood and powerlessness. We look to authority figures to solve our problems and make us feel better. We believe others are doing things to us. Tamas spirituality is either non-existent or is very rule-based and fundamental. If tamas predominates in a person, they will feel insecure and powerless, so religions providing clear rules and simple divisions between good and bad offer a lifeline of stability in a world of chaos. The motto of tamas is: "I can't".

Rajas is the stage of empowerment. In this stage, we discover that we have some control over how we feel and we begin taking responsibility for our inner states. We discover the power of intent and we give ourselves over to ambitions and worthy tasks. This is the home of self-improvement, coaching, management, leadership and anything that concerns itself with bettering the self and society. Rajasic spirituality is about climbing the ladder of achievement to a state of bliss. It involves rules for achieving spiritual outcomes and might include complex theologies, with elaborate attempts to fit non-rational events into rational and intellectual structures. In rajas, spirituality is debated and codified. Contrast this with tamas spirituality, where truths are written in stone and handed down to be followed verbatim.

The great dream of rajas is for a better world and an improved self. The motto of rajas is "I can". Teachers of this stage will say things like: "Anything you set your mind to you can achieve!" The hoped-for result is an enlightened self, but the true result is a perfected, highly functioning ego.

Sattva is the stage of surrender and wisdom. You are surrendering the small self, the ego, to the reality of the greater Life that is living through you and as you. In sattva, you begin to let go of some of your big ambitions, even your spiritual ambitions, as you realise that whatever you have achieved has not brought you the peace and union you so desire. The mark of the sattvic life is surrender of attachment to outcomes. The motto of sattva is the same as that for tamas – "I can't" – but it has a completely different meaning. It is the recognition of the powerlessness of the ego to create change. It is the insight that change is less about your doing than about the greater Life that is living through you. A great expression of this is, "Not my will but thine be done." If Jesus was an Empowerment teacher, he would have tried to affirm the crucifixion away. But he wasn't. His teaching was based in sattva and in a further stage, which I will explain in a moment.

Sattvic spirituality is about meditation, yoga, mystical contemplation and mindfulness practices. There are few rules and precepts and very little theology, if any. Sattvic spirituality is practical and aims at a direct experience of God, the All.

Instead of using the terms tamas, rajas and sattva I will often use the terms Victimhood, Empowerment and Wisdom. For Wisdom I also sometimes use the word "Surrender" because you are essentially surrendering the ego will for the greater will of Life that is living through you and as you.

In some teachings, the sattvic conditions of peacefulness, joy and wisdom are viewed as the pinnacle of achievement. However, in the Gita, Krishna tells Arjuna that sattva is still just a facet of the created world and that the true home of the gods is beyond the gunas. Arjuna asks him how one might recognise someone who has gone beyond the gunas, and Krishna tells him that no matter which guna arises, such a person will neither dislike its presence nor desire it when it is not there. The one who has transcended the gunas is content with whatever happens and sees dirt, rocks and gold as equal. Such a one is serene in success and failure, unperturbed by any phenomena that appear in awareness.

To transcend the gunas, we need to be aware of our attachments to them. When rajas predominates we are attached to action and to outcomes. When sattva predominates, we are attached to wisdom and happiness. The lesson here (and the central one of this book) is that even wisdom and happiness have to be transcended if we are to know true joy and peace.

We can now add a fourth stage of development to our topology. If Stage 1 is Victimhood, Stage 2 is Empowerment and Stage 3 is Wisdom, then Stage 4 is Unity. Unity begins with the realisation that one is not identified by any passing states or moods, whether negative or positive. Identity becomes increasingly associated with pure, trans-personal Being as consciousness becomes more and more nondual in nature.

I will use this topology of the four stages of development throughout this book. The point I want to make in this chapter is simply that your pain about your apparent non-achievement in your material, emotional and spiritual ambitions can be lessened considerably if you consider where you are in the stages of development. If you are reading this book, chances are good that you have a good education and have done some inner work and self-improvement. This means you will have unconsciously adopted the precepts of rajas Empowerment, which is the energy behind Western-style industrialisation and scientific advancement. It is put out there by most of the popular teachers that this stage of Empowerment and improvement is the ultimate stage – that it just goes on forever, with things getting better and better until it's all truly awesome and everyone is happy. If you have been following these teachings and absorbing these expectations from society, it's no wonder you are feeling a bit let down by reality. For as you've just seen, Empowerment is not the end, and the assumption of eternal progress is a myth. At some point, everything that has been built up through the energy of rajas and the will of the self must be surrendered so that truth can prevail. The truth, at least for this part of the journey, is the realisation that the small self is illusory and has no power. Just when you thought you were finally getting it right and were about to meet God or achieve your spiritual dreams – it all fell apart. What they didn't tell you when you signed up for this was that this breakdown was to be expected. That's because many of the teachers out there haven't been through this yet and don't know about it. But you have, or you are in the middle of it right now.

Consider this – your failings are not telling you about something you are doing wrong, they are telling you that you're on track. The system of Empowerment is designed to fail because it is based on a false premise – the notion that there is a separate "I" inside you who is doing all this. Consider that perhaps you are failing at Empowerment for the good reason that you are moving over to the next stage, which is Wisdom consciousness. The transition can be hugely disconcerting. In fact, I place the first Dark Night of the Soul at this point. The second comes at the transition from Wisdom to Union.

For now, simply allow your distress at your apparent failings to come to rest in the knowledge that you are not doing anything wrong or failing in any way. In fact, things are right on schedule for your awakening to the next phase of your journey. This book is a guide for your transition from rajas to sattva, from Empowerment to Surrender and beyond.

The inside-out model

From this discussion on the stages of spiritual development we can now see that the existing model of self-improvement is very much an Empowerment project. As such it is really a huge improvement on Victim consciousness, but it is not the end of the road. To create a new model that will support true happiness and joy, we need to forge onward into Wisdom and perhaps even Unity consciousness.

So let's get started!

If we call the old model the outside-in model or the Law of Materialism, let's call the new one the inside-out model or the Law of Emergence. I introduced the Law of Emergence a bit earlier, so you already know some of the insights from it. Under the Law of Emergence, we do not have to seek the good outside of ourselves and we do not need to improve ourselves or fix ourselves, for we are already whole and complete. The splits in the shell of the acorn do not indicate its failure to be an acorn; they indicate that something greater than the acorn is ready to be born through it. The model of Emergence says that we do not have to go out and get our greatness, we simply have to allow it to emerge. In fact, any attempts to get something – and this often involves us trying to fix ourselves and better ourselves – merely obscure the

35

perfection that we are already. (Later in this book I will outline how self-improvement and creating change can be accommodated in the Emergence model, but let's just keep it simple for now.)

The outside-in model, or Law of Materialism, is based on rigid individualism – the notion that you are a separate self that has to apply itself to growing and learning and breaking free. In the inside-out model, however, you recognise that life is expressing itself through you and as you, and that your interference in this process is not required. All you need to do is to tune in to what is already happening with you and to allow it, cultivate it and say yes to it. Your work is to say yes to God's yes. God, Life, is doing all the work. You do not need to intend and create, for anything you do from the position of a separate self will end up being an ego creation that will not meet your deeper needs. In the Law of Emergence your work of intention is simply to create the inner conditions that support the unfolding of Life's intentions. Ultimately, it's not even true to say that your work is to do anything because that still implies a doer who is separate from what is done. However, we don't need to go that far down the rabbit hole to begin to harness the power of Emergence.

Now this message of Life living through you and as you will be difficult for the ego to hear, but it is music to the soul. It is the relief and the peace that you have been looking for. You do not have to succeed or get it right. The "you" that wants to succeed will never succeed, for in wanting something it is affirming that it is not what it wants.

This does not mean that you suppress your wants, for that is impossible. It means that you listen to your wants and let them guide you to the fullness that is beneath the wanting. You can only want what you already have. If you want love, simply be with this wanting without rushing out to try and get someone to fulfil your need. Your need is not going to be fulfilled by someone, it is going to be fulfilled by you. This is the secret of true happiness in life. When you create in this way you are unattached to outcomes because you know you have already achieved your goal and the physical manifestation of love and wealth is merely a reflection of something that has already happened within you.

The principles of Emergence

The basic premise of the Emergence model is that you are already what you are seeking. You are it. In the rest of this chapter I will outline some more of the principles of Emergence.

1. Inner states are independent of outer conditions

In the materialist understanding of the outside-in model, we have to arrange our outer circumstances to bring us happiness and security. When unwanted things happen we feel justified in feeling bad, and when wanted things happen we naturally feel happy. In this system, mastery is defined as the ability to manipulate one's environment to bring more good than bad. However, no matter how masterful one gets at creating one's outer reality, things still go wrong and bad feelings still come to visit.

By contrast, when one is living from the inside-out understanding, one knows that circumstances are always in flux and that good follows bad and bad follows good. So instead of trying to manipulate outer conditions to create desired inner conditions, we go straight to the core of it and create our own inner states.

Remember the Feeling Fallacy again. Our feelings are the result of our thinking, not of the world. It is our thinking that determines how we feel.

So far so good, but I want to take things a bit deeper. You see, after reading what I've just written you might recognise the Law of Attraction teachings that advise us to change our thinking so that we raise our vibration to match whatever it is we want to create. In my mind, this is a great first step. But it's still in the realm of outside-in. It's saying that I must create or manipulate something (my thoughts) so that I can feel better inside. Outside-in. The belief is that if I just change my thoughts, I can change my life. This is great – but just look at all the "I" and "me" in there. We are still asleep in the dream.

So what's the alternative?

The alternative is to acknowledge that you are not just this little me, this "I" who must act against the world and against its own thoughts. You are greater than that. In fact, so great that you are not even you anymore. There is a deeper level of your being that is truly transpersonal – it is no longer yours alone. Think of it as the undercurrent of the universe, or as Life itself, or as God or Nature. I like to call it Being. This is what we are going to rely on to create our inner conditions, not our puny mind with its fragile willpower.

So here's what we do. We simply stop, notice we are feeling bad about something, and recognise that this feeling is coming from some or other thought or belief. We don't even need to know what that thought is. We just observe, and we leave everything alone. The act of non-judgemental observation is a powerful medicine that comes from beyond the separate self. The you who is observing is not the ego you – it is something that is not at all invested in the good and bad of things. It just is. When you observe from this place and simply be with yourself in a compassionate way, something shifts. The uncomfortable feeling starts to lift. It might even communicate with you, telling you what it wants. As you listen, you are effortlessly doing the work of transmutation, turning the lead of misunderstanding and hurt into the gold of insight and loving kindness.

If you wrestle with your thoughts and try to turn them into better thoughts, you are buying into the dream world. You are perfecting the dream. But you don't want that anymore, do you? You are interested in waking up from the dream. To do that you need to stop doing dream things like changing how you think.

Please note I am not saying you never change your thoughts to be more positive, for I do this all the time. It's just that there is a time and place for everything. If you catch yourself in the moment thinking bad things about a person or situation, by all means stop doing that and find something positive. Dream the best dream you can. It's just that if you are wanting to go deeper to the realm of transformation, and if you are wanting to awaken from the dream, then you might want to try this new way of letting all interference go and falling into the underlying positivity of Life itself.

In the inside-out world, mastery is gaining the ability to be OK with yourself regardless of circumstances. It is not about always feeling good, it is about ending the struggle to make things better and discovering the freedom that is always present as your true nature.

Viktor Frankl, a psychiatrist who survived the Nazi concentration camps, devoted the rest of his life to understanding what happened in the camps and how some prisoners managed to survive while others perished. He found that it all came down to meaning. Those who stood the best chance of survival had found some kind of meaning that transcended the dire conditions in which they lived. He ends his book "The Will to Meaning" with the following quote from the book of Habakkuk, which I quote again here. It is a pure expression of the enlightened, inside-out approach that triumphs over all circumstances. And once again, substitute the word "God" with "Life" or whatever has meaning for you.

> For even if the fig tree does not blossom,
> and no fruit is on the vines,
> even if the olive tree fails to produce,
> and the fields yield no food,
> even if the sheep vanish from the sheep pen,
> and there are no cows in the stalls;
> still, I will rejoice in God,
> I will take joy in the God of my salvation.
> God is my strength!
> He makes me swift and sure-footed as a deer
> so I may walk on the steep mountains.
>
> Habakkuk 3:17-19

2. We are not here to get something but to give something

We often find ourselves praying for something or seeking answers to our problems. This is a way we learnt in childhood – when we needed something we asked an adult. The source of nourishment and supply was outside of ourselves. Now in adulthood we find we continue to operate on the same model. When things become challenging or we feel the pain of some or other lack, we ask what we must do to fill the empty space. We live as if we were looking for the answer to a prayer.

But what if we have come here not to seek answers to our prayers but to be the answer to a prayer? If we lack nothing in our true nature and we are here to express the fullness of being, then we are already the answer we seek. Consider simply that you have come as the answer to a prayer. In your ordinary daily activities you are answering the prayer of how to live as a fully human, fully divine expression of the One. Even with all your perceived faults in place, you are a full and complete expression of the One.

So the question is, what prayer are you an answer to?

You are an answer to the prayers that you pray. You are an answer to the questions you ask. Even when no answers come, your asking and then living from the place of the question becomes your giving of the answer. The answer is your life, lived. The light you have been seeking is your very life, as you are living it. You are the answer of how to live a challenging life with integrity. You are the answer of how to love yourself and the world when all you encounter is opposition and lovelessness. You are an answer to all your questions, even when you appear to fail. The One does not recognise failure, for everything that appears is an equal expression of the One. The One does not know the answer until you give it.

Does your heart long to believe this, even if your mind objects? That longing is the calling of your truth. You know you are not a mistake, though you often feel that way. You know deep down that you are divine, no matter what is happening in your world. Do you think Jesus felt like a million bucks when he was on the cross? No, I should imagine he was having a pretty rough time. But beneath the suffering of the body was the divine knowing that even this was right, that it could be no other way. Father, why have you forsaken me? The crucifixion becomes the lived answer. God has not forsaken you, for see, even though you suffer this pain, you are loving those who persecute you. You have seen the divinity in them, even as you find it within yourself. Fully human, fully divine.

Consider now that you are the answer to your prayers. That means that how you live your current challenges is the answer. You do not have to worry about how to get down off your cross, you simply have to live your circumstances with authenticity and with an inward focus on that which is ever beyond circumstance.

In the Emergence model we throw out concepts like "getting it right" and "succeeding". We begin with the success you already are. The light you seek is your life, lived.

3. Pray *from* abundance, not *for* abundance

We are used to looking at prayer as asking God, Universe or whatever for guidance or for some favour. Even if you don't relate to any god-concept, you might find yourself inwardly asking for something or intending something that will fill some kind of lack. All these forms of prayer are based on lack and an outside-in interpretation of reality. At its core is the belief that one's good is out there somewhere and someone or something must bring it to one. Prayer and intention that comes from this understanding is riddled with the very lack and powerlessness it seeks to overcome. No wonder such prayer doesn't usually work.

In the inside-out understanding of the Emergence model, prayer is about expressing what you already have. You are not praying for something that seems to be missing, you are praying from your already existing state of fullness. You are asking how you might express, give and share more of what you have within you. So instead of asking for the partner of your dreams, you get in touch with your own inner condition of love, generosity and wellbeing and you ask how this might be expressed in the world. You begin by loving yourself and finding within you the affirmation, support and tenderness that you have been seeking from another. You meet yourself in your loneliness and offer yourself compassion and warmth and care. You find the place that knows you are not alone, even if right now your circumstances seem to provide evidence of your aloneness. Then from this inner state of having, you can ask yourself how this havingness might like to express itself in the world. Or perhaps, from this place of already possessing what you seek, you discover you are no longer as driven to achieve your outer goal and will find some peace about it. When you no longer *need* a relationship (as opposed to *loving* to have one), you regain the power you were giving away in trying to find a relationship. If you met someone in this state of lacking you would find yourself doing things that went against your inner values just to keep the relationship going. Powerlessness and unbalanced compromise will not bring you what you seek.

The same goes for money and any other condition. For example, this morning I found myself in a state of emptiness and challenge. It being a Monday, I woke up to the realisation that I had few clients lined up and no other work in the pipeline. I began to feel the nagging voices of lack and fear. My old friend, the "what must I do?" thought began to knock loudly at the door. So what I did was I recognised that I was falling into the illusion of lack and that if I carried on listening to the so-called evidence I would really begin believing I was in trouble. So I sat quietly with these feelings, noticing a certain scratchiness and irritation in my energy. I did not try to change anything; I just noticed and allowed it, giving myself the compassionate care I was needing. After a while I began to feel both the discomfort of what I lacked and the comfort of true Being. I tuned into Being and allowed it to fill me. Then from this fullness I asked how I might share this good feeling with the world. I didn't have any clients booked, so I couldn't immediately share it with them, but I remembered the obvious, which was that I was writing a book! Through the book I could reach many more people than just seeing individual clients. I got up and went to my desk and started writing. Right now, in the background, I can still feel some of the uncertainty and fear about what to do to get financial flow happening, but I am also deeply in the flow as I write this. I have faith that the flow will lead where I need to go.

Do not pray for what you need, pray from the place of having what you need, that what you have may be expressed and shared with everyone. You are truly the light of the world.

4. You created all of this

This morning I was meditating and I found my mind drifting towards a persistent problem that had been bugging me for years. I found myself wondering how I should go about resolving it. A feeling of defeat came over me because I remembered all the other times I had prayed on this subject and affirmed on it or intended on it or surrendered on it ... and still there was no shift. Like countless others before me who have faced things they could not change I sat there and asked, "God, Self, anybody, tell me now – what must I do?"

And, of course, there was no answer. But what did happen next surprised me. I suddenly realised that in praying and intending and doing all this stuff to fix a problem I was assuming that somebody else – God, universe, Life – had created it. But what if I had created it all? I knew then with a very direct sense of certainty that I was creating everything, even if I didn't know how or why I was doing this. Clearly, it was not the conscious self who was doing the creating, but the greater I was behind all of it. How could it not be? If everything is one, then there is only one creator, and in my world that is me. Not the little me, but the me that is all things. I don't know if I'm getting across what I felt in that moment because I know I have heard this same message before and it didn't really sink in ... but this morning it really came home. This is all me. The problem is not separate from me. I have created the situation to wake me up. Actually, I don't know why I created it, but if I did create it, and I know I did, it must be for a good reason.

Now you might immediately start thinking, well if we are creating it, let's throw in some affirmations and visualisations and shift this thing. But that is once again treating it with the outside-in approach, which says we have to do something to get something. What if the work is simply to recognise that one has created everything and that it is therefore a conspiracy of benevolence to wake one up from the dream? What if fixing wasn't the goal, but awakening was?

In the moment I had this realisation I did not feel the call to go and change anything. Instead I felt a sense of pure power and joy. I was making all of this up ... how amazing! I cannot tell you what a difference it makes to recognise that the so-called problem is not outside yourself but is actually within. It means the problem is still there, but you are no longer at odds with it. You no longer feel life is doing something to you (outside-in). Rather, you have discovered union with your circumstances. Just the knowing that it's an inside-out job brings great relief.

Right now as I think about the issue I was wrestling with I no longer feel so blocked on it. I still don't know what to do about it, but that feeling is not so harsh anymore. The whole setup has a kindness and benevolence to it. I don't have to figure out how to solve it because I created it. This doesn't mean I have to somehow figure out what I meant when I created it, I can simply surrender to the same force that created the situation. The I that created the problem must have the solution. That's all I need to know. And besides, from this perspective, is it really a problem anymore? I prefer to think of it as a conspiracy of grace, a mystery of awakening.

So right now, before you go on to the next principle, perhaps you would like to spend a few moments considering those things in your life that seem like problems. And then ask yourself: What if I have actually created all of this to achieve something good? What if I am really at cause here, even if I don't yet know why I did this?

Does this perspective change things for you?

5. Your wants and needs point to what you already have, not to what is missing

Under the theory of Materialism, our needs indicate something that is missing in our lives. We believe we have to go out into the world and find something that we don't already have.

Under the model of Emergence, however, our needs indicate something that we already are that wants to emerge. If we feel a need for love, that need is coming from the love we already have. The pain we feel is because we are looking in the wrong place for love. Remember the Feeling Fallacy? Our bad feeling about not having a partner is not telling us about a true condition in the world, it is telling us about our interpretation of a neutral set of circumstances. The pain is not because we are separate from love but because we think we are. Feeling is generated by thinking or beliefs, not by the world.

When we encounter a need we become aware of something that seems to be missing, and then we set out into the world to find it. But of course we never do. So what usually happens is that we continue seeking (craving), or we go the opposite way (avoidance) and develop a philosophy that says needs are bad and should be transcended. But this is a partial truth, created in a moment of reaction. While it is true that feelings of lack are misinterpretations of reality, if we simply repress them and pretend to be beyond needs we will not awaken to the truth that lies beneath them. The truth is that you are what you seek. If you deny that you have needs then you become divorced from the source of those needs, which is the fullness of Being.

46

The pain of what is missing is a doorway to what is never missing.

Have faith in the pain of loss, for at its core is the fullness of Being that you seek.

So how might you discover this?

As with all processes in this book, it begins with stopping all craving and avoidance. Stop chasing after something that will fill the emptiness, and stop denying the emptiness. Just be with the discomfort. Become present to what appears to be missing in your life, whether that be love, wealth, appreciation, or anything else. You be with it, meaning you do not run towards a solution or run away from it by indulging in some addiction. You just sit with the longing. We find that when we are present to our longings, at some point they give way to the fullness that is beneath them. The longing for love turns out to be the yearning for our own love to be expressed and to be received in the world. Our desire for material wealth is our desire to know and recognise our own value and worth. When we are in touch with this elemental fullness and state of having, we can then flow back into the world and allow the expression of our inner truth to unfold.

I'll slow this technique down into much greater detail in the next chapter. For now, simply remember the model of Emergence regards needs as indicators of what you are, not of what is missing.

6. Whatever is in the way, is the way

In the conventional model, obstacles, blocks and other kinds of opposition are things that have to be tackled head-on and solved. Obstacles are things that stand in the way of us achieving what we think we need to achieve. They are indicative of something wrong that needs to be set right. A lot of coaching modalities focus on helping people overcome their blocks to success. The person is here and success is over there, and inbetween is this pesky thing called a block. See the duality in this?

So now we must ask, if our greatness is already within us and if we are already a whole expression of the One, is this so-called block really separate from me? Can it really be in opposition to my purpose?

Before we consider another way of looking at blocks and obstacles, let's have a bit of a story. Long, long ago, long before humans were around, the world was ruled by giant lizards. Today we call them dinosaurs. These dinosaurs inhabited the earth for millions of years. Things looked pretty good for them, until one sad day when something utterly disastrous happened. A giant meteor crashed into the earth, creating such havoc that it changed the world's climate for a long time. The dinosaurs could no longer survive in this terrible new world, and so they died out. It was a tragedy of unimaginable proportions. Life after the great extinction was very different to what it was before. Animals were smaller, more timid. Silly creatures like apes began to appear and to thrive. After a long time, one of these apes evolved into something we call a human, and now humans rule the world. The tragedy of the dinosaurs made way for the birth of a higher life form and the arrival of self-aware consciousness on the planet. So the question is this: was the arrival of the asteroid or whatever it was that destroyed the dinosaurs really a bad thing?

In the greater unfolding of life on earth, the old way had to make way for something unimaginable. What at first seemed like an obstacle to life became the herald of a whole new order of life at a far higher level of development.

Under the model of Emergence, whatever is in the way is embraced not as an obstacle to the path but as the path itself.

Obstacles and blocks are saying that there is something trying to emerge in you that is more than you can imagine. The block is indicating that you are living in a world that is too small for your grander intentions.

When the caterpillar loses interest in eating leaves and just wants to curl up into a cocoon and do nothing, is this desire really a block to her caterpillar success? Something the caterpillar could never imagine is about to be born through her. If she fights against it by regarding the transformation as a block she will be standing against her own evolution. For here's the thing, the greatness that you are and that wants to be born through you and as you is often unimaginable to the conscious mind. You see, your imagination is part of your conscious mind, or part of what is already known. Yes, your imagination seems to give you new things, but it is creating them from known ingredients. To really let something new be born through you, you have to go to a deeper realm, what we call the realm of visioning. Visioning is receiving impulses from the ground of Being, from the greater you. If the caterpillar must imagine her ideal life she will imagine being the biggest and bestest caterpillar in the forest. But her true destiny is not in her existing experience, it is beyond it. So when this destiny approaches it feels like something unwanted and alarming. Consider that whatever in your life is not working and is resisting your attempts to fix is simply the equivalent of the caterpillar trying to fix her caterpillar life. What might happen if you stop with the fixing and go with the flow that is already happening?

As a way of guiding this inquiry, let's do it step by step:

1. Stop doing whatever you are doing to try and get through the block.

2. Feel the block fully and make peace with the fact that it is there (say yes to present experience).

3. Ask yourself Emergence questions such as: If I let go of trying to make things work, what would I really love to do? How am I playing too small in my life right now? What is the highest vision of this work that is trying to emerge? And, what quality do I need to embrace to be truly free in this moment?

4. Be open to the impulses that come to you. Follow the inspiration.

I want to give you another quick example from my own life. For years I have been feeling blocked on writing another novel. I have sketches for about five novels lying around, but nothing is taking shape. I have been through extreme frustration with this, because just as I thought my career as a novelist was about to take off, things crashed. However, what has emerged from that so-called block was the work I am currently telling you about. What has also emerged is this very book. If I were writing novels I would be thinking of myself as a novelist and I wouldn't be going deeper on this subject and reaching people with the message I long to express. It could be that I will get back to writing fiction again, but it will be in a different way to what I had imagined before. The point is that sometimes your plans are stopped so that something you could not have imagined can be born through you and as you. Sometimes your beloved plans are forged by your dear, sweet ego, and so if your deepest value is truth, then these fantasy goals will inevitably perish. Whatever is in the way, is the way. It is all a conspiracy of grace to awaken us to that which our limited intelligence can barely imagine.

7. Visualisation has its limits

If you have been following the Law of Attraction teachings you will probably have heard a lot about the power of visualisation. Visualisation is the process of creating a clear picture in our minds of what we want to achieve. We make the picture as vivid as possible, adding the colours, the sights, the sounds and the textures of how life will be when we have achieved our goal. As a hypnotherapist I know the value of visualisation in creating positive expectation in people and, perhaps most importantly, laying down new neural pathways that support new habits and outlooks on life. You see, the inner mind does not distinguish between a real experience and an imagined one, so if you imagine something clearly, your biochemical and electrical systems react to the imagined situation as if you were experiencing it in real life. You only have to look to your fears to see how imagined outcomes are taken by the body as real. The power of visualisation is that when you imagine yourself doing something, your brain takes the new activity as real and starts laying down the neural connections that support this new skill. So you really can programme your mind to do things differently. Imagine how your life will be different when you know that you can change your perceptions and the content of your life by visualising and imagining positive outcomes. If you're not already doing this, you might want to give it a try.

Now you're waiting for the catch.

Well, let's just put it this way – visualising an outcome is a giant leap towards causeless joy because you are leaving outside evidence alone and you are focusing on how you want things to be. If you are feeling poor, just visualise your ideal paycheck and immerse yourself in the imagined feeling of abundance. When you do this, your brain starts sifting through all the incoming data and starts bringing you evidence of the wealth that already exists in your life. And somewhere in this data there will be an opportunity for you, and because you are now feeling more positive you will be able to recognise it and grab it. That's the Law of Attraction at work.

So why am I saying it's just a leap towards causeless joy and not actual causeless joy?

Well, perhaps you can answer this yourself. In the scheme of Victimhood, Empowerment and Wisdom, where would you place visualisation and conscious intention?

I would place it right there in the middle – at Empowerment. You are not just lying around like a victim, you are actively changing your circumstances. In this case, you are changing your internal circumstances – your thoughts and feelings – to create an outer effect. So it's clearly Empowerment. While it has one foot in the door of the inside-out understanding, it still saying that this moment of now is not where we want to be, and that over there is a better place, a better feeling, a better thought. We are still in the realm of manipulating reality to achieve something that we want. It's kind of like enlightened Empowerment, or as author and coach Michael Neill calls it, enlightened outside-in. If you're doing this regularly then you're doing really well and can consider yourself on a path of true self-actualization. It's just that if this is all you're doing, you might encounter some limitations.

The main limitation is that when you use visualisation you are going into your imagination to rearrange what you already know. You decide you want to be a great golfer, so you get into a quiet state and visualise your swings and putts. Or you decide to manifest a house by the sea, so you go in and do all the fun work of imagining your ideal home and then you see what action steps flow from that empowered vision. So far so good ... but it's still more of *you*. More of what you know. More of you being in control.

As you will have discovered in this book so far, where we are going is beyond who we are and what we know. The caterpillar can spend every one of her hours visualising the perfect caterpillar existence, eating only organic leaves, and having perfectly conditioned hair that glints in the sun, but that's all going to be for nothing. Her destiny is not in the realm of her imagination, it is in the realm of Emergence. The greater intelligence that makes oak trees from acorns and butterflies from caterpillars has other plans for our hairy friend.

There comes a time when we must let go of visualisation and surrender to a deeper call that comes from beyond our imagination. To do this, we use a process that I borrow from Michael Beckwith called visioning. In visioning, we enter a positive space within ourselves, just as we do with visualisation, but instead of creating an outcome we simply invite a response from life and listen to what shows up. We open to that which wants to come to us. This is active surrender. Our work is to create the conditions necessary to hear the call that comes from beyond our limited imagination. We let go of what we think we want and become open to what the soul wants. By soul I mean that deeper part of you that is aligned with the All, that flows with cosmic intention rather than personal intention.

While Visualisation is classic Stage 2 Empowerment, visioning is part of Stage 3, which I have called Wisdom consciousness, and which some also call Channel or Surrender consciousness. You become a channel for Life itself. Your job is not to create but to open to the creation that wants to take shape through you and as you. The work is to create the vessel for Spirit to fill. To get to this stage you have to be at that point where you know that no matter how much more you manifest and intend and visualise, you're still not going to get what you want and your life is still going to be full of ups and downs. At this point, life becomes about service to the greater good and to the intentions of Life itself.

Not my will but thine be done.

53

Are you ready to say this in your life?

That is what the world's great teachers have been gently pointing us towards. And yes, it's not easy to let go of what the small self wants. If we are busy manifesting the life of our dreams, we aren't going to be open to this message. That's why we sometimes need something like a meteor to come crashing into our lives so it disrupts the old pattern and opens us to something unexpected. This point is the true Dark Night of the Soul. All your petty endeavours are stripped away so that you can finally awaken to the illusion of your life. Not my will but thine be done. Again and again, if you are on this path, you will be brought back to this point where you surrender your will to the will of the divine. It is not the surrender of tamas, which just couldn't be bothered. It is the surrender, often in deep pain, of the life you thought you had to live in order to be happy. The divine is saying that all that stuff is window dressing. If you want to know the true peace and happiness, throw away all that can be built up through time and stay with what is here now. You can see how easily that message can be misinterpreted, so you don't need to go and give away your house and job and go live in a commune. This is simply saying that you shouldn't depend on these things to give you joy, because the eternal joy you seek is already here, simply unrecognised. We get to discover that when things don't go our way and we lose things that we thought were essential to our happiness. When we surrender to this present joy, the essence of joy naturally unfolds into the manifestation of abundance and wellbeing that is most beneficial to us. It might not look the way we wanted it to, but it will be what we wanted deep down.

8. Embrace what seems broken

Remember my story of the dinosaurs and how they were wiped out by a meteor, at least according to one theory? If dinosaurs were capable of visualising and intending, there's no way they would have intended such an event or imagined its outcome. Or let's think of forest fires that burn down large tracts of forest and result in the deaths of countless creatures. If the creatures had to get into visualising their ideal lives they would never have included anything as violent as a fire, and yet we now know that for certain types of forests to thrive, they need to experience fire.

Visualisation does not include the meteors that bring our old existence to an end or the forest fires that clear out the old growth so that something new can emerge. Whenever we visualise and intend we try to create a world without the disasters that bring new life. But the challenges that we try to avoid are preparing us for what we most want.

This principle is really a restatement of the principle that whatever is in the way, is the way. The obstacles are not signs of failure to grow, they are inseparable from the very growth you seek. If you just let go of active visualising for a while and go into the deeper process of visioning, you will better be able to incorporate those dramatic and devastating occurrences that sweep through your life and seem to destroy what is most valuable to you. Life is conspiring to wake you up to the truth that you already have everything you need, even if you can't see it right now. Sometimes, what we thought we needed was simply a distraction from what we really needed.

If you are facing a forest fire in your life, or an arctic winter, let go into it and open to the possibility that it is here to serve your evolution. Your task is not to put out the fire, it is to undergo the transmutation that it brings. What is trying to be born through you that can only be born if the old is allowed to perish?

9. Action does not cause change – it *is* the change

We are taught from early on that action gets things going. We need to do things to get things. And this really works, up to a point. The point is the discovery that no matter how much we do, we are still not getting what we really want. You see, if doing and acting is all we are doing, then we are operating on the principle that something has to be created that wasn't there before. We see a situation of lack, and then we do something to fill it. This involves a lot of effort. For many of us, effort is absolutely necessary for achieving anything worthwhile. We have absorbed this belief from just about everyone in society. And if we look over there at those people who are making no effort, all we see are slackers and layabouts. What's really happening is that we are equating effortlessness with tamasic avoidance, while really they are poles apart. Effort gets us into Empowerment, so it is the antidote to slothful slacking. But effort also leads to overwork and to the discovery that one still has not achieved one's ambitions. One solution is to go forward into a more enlightened kind of slacking, which we can call simply being.

In a state of being, we are active, alert and awake to opportunities. We flow with the forces of creation. In the outside-in model, we are acting to make things happen. In the inside-out model, we are acting to confirm what is true already. Acting doesn't make change happen, it simply locks in the fact that change has already happened. Acting is meant to demonstrate an already-existing state of being and to allow us to experience the unfolding of a timeless creation in time. Action makes real what being already possesses.

4. ACCESSING THE REALM OF CAUSELESS JOY

This is where we get to talk about techniques. The world of coaching and self-development is full of techniques for achieving success and overcoming obstacles, but we are concerned with something different. We are looking for the peace and the joy that are independent of circumstances and the whole rigmarole of getting things right and improving things. We are longing for Wisdom consciousness and, even deeper than that, for Unity consciousness. When we get to these realms it becomes somewhat tricky to talk about techniques and practices because there can be no process for attaining that which is always and ever present. Conventionally, we perform practices or do techniques to get something that is not here right now. We forget that the very act of doing a technique is itself inseparable from that which it seeks to achieve. From this level of understanding, there is simply nothing to be done. And yet, paradoxically, if we do nothing without first having this understanding, nothing happens.

The key is to engage in these practices in the spirit of inquiry – an investigation into what is here right now, rather than an attempt to shift something or get somewhere. When we practise from this understanding we are harnessing the power of Being. Being is pure consciousness that is aware of itself. Being does not just sit and do nothing, its nature is to inquire. One might say that inquiry is an unfolding of that which already is. It is not going anywhere, and yet it is unfolding. If you actively do nothing because you believe no technique can get you to what you already are, you are denying inquiry and the flow of Being, but if you actively do something to achieve an outcome, you are employing ego. The place we want to work from is neither avoidance nor craving but rather a curious inquiry into the truth of this moment. As the Zen Buddhists say, we practise because that's what Buddhas do. The very act of practice and inquiry is the enlightenment we seek.

All right, enough of that, let's get into the practical stuff.

I am going to outline something I call the Presence Shift Process. This is about stopping all our seeking for something better and saying yes to what is here right now. We say yes to our happiness, our pain, our discomfort. The yes is the doorway to the present moment. In the present, we are nonresistant to experience, and in the ease of this nonresistance we become aware of Presence. Presence is our felt sense of Being. This essential being is often experienced as causeless joy. It has other qualities as well, such as love, compassion, peace, rootedness and ruthless truth. This morning I heard someone experience it as pure intelligence. This essential nature is the true medicine we are seeking. When we live from here, solutions become apparent that weren't available before. When we no longer see problems, problem situations have a way of resolving themselves.

The Presence Shift process

Most of the feel-good strategies out there advise you to reach for a good feeling whenever you feel down. Now there is some merit in this, but I've already pointed out that while you can get temporary benefit from it, it is not usually transformative. To transform and to grow you've got to meet and allow all the disowned and disgruntled and distressed parts of you, as well as all the good-feeling parts. As we will discover, there is a "good" that lies beyond all good and bad feeling, and this is what we are in the process of discovering.

Let's do a quick experiment to demonstrate this: Picture yourself standing or sitting in a pleasant scene; it could be outside or inside. Now imagine two figures approach you. They are children, and when you look closely you see they look very much like you did when you were young. You notice also that one of the children is clean, healthy, happy and confident. The other is dirty, sickly and somewhat hostile. Maybe this one swears or cries or even starts causing trouble with the other one.

Now imagine you get up and in a stern voice command the dirty, troubled one to be gone. "Go away, I never want to see you again. I am the light and only the light. You, miserable, dark creature, get back to where you came from!"

OK, feel the energy of that?

Now reset the scene with these two children, the troubled one and the happy one. See them both before you. Breathe into your heart and absorb the energies of both these children. Now follow what your heart wants to do in relation to these children.

Really do spend some time with this.

So ... what happened?

I'm willing to bet that you didn't banish the unhappy one. Perhaps you simply allowed them to enter your space and you listened to them. Or maybe your heart opened and you felt yourself giving them an embrace.

My question is this: Which scene evoked the best in you – the one where you banished the troubled child or the one where you welcomed it?

Do you see the hurt we do ourselves when we banish our dark selves? It is our own child self we are banishing. The dear and brave one who dared to love and got hurt in the process. And now we are rejecting them. It was bad enough when the world rejected them, but now we are doing it to ourselves. No wonder we suffer!

So here is the core of my technique: Make welcome every appearance of your own dear self. Make place for the happy, the joyful, the sad, the angry, the failed, the depressed, the successful, the playful, the serious ... make space for all of you. Then, in this space of allowing and experiencing, notice the qualities of Being that begin to show themselves. Even though there is pain and discomfort and resistance, there is also joy and peace and stillness. When unnameable Being emerges into the world it expresses itself as the ineffable qualities of joy, peace, compassion, stillness, truth and power, amongst others. Sometimes I refer to these flavours or qualities of Being as essence qualities. We can speak of the essence of joy or peace or strength. When we recognise and tune into these essences or qualities of Being, we exist less as personality and more as Presence. Presence is who we are in the timeless moment of now. We flow with the will of Life itself.

All right, let's put this into some kind of a process:

1. Stop fixing

2. Allow present experience and really feel it

3. Shift into Presence

4. Open to action steps

Step 1: Stop fixing

The first step is to stop trying to fix your problem or making yourself feel better. You are fighting against yourself, so just stop everything.

Step 2: Allow present experience

Once you have stopped your strategies to avoid the pain, allow the pain in, or whatever other sensation is most real for you in this moment. Really feel it. If you are feeling something quite intense, it can help to breathe into the pain, trouble or discomfort, absorbing more of it with the in-breath and then just noticing it on the out-breath. By breathing it in we make space for it and halt the automatic avoidance we've been indulging in. When we avoid pain we buy into its reality, so this step is about detaching from the story and from the illusion of good and bad.

If you are really feeling triggered and in a bit of a state, you might want to give yourself plenty of time on this part of the process. We'll call this step the step of Allowing. We can also call it "finding the yes to present experience". In saying yes to what is here we end our struggle with reality. We think we have to fight against the dark, but if the dark is already here, then it is also Life and our work is to allow and say yes to it. This might also trigger you a little and bring up the belief that if you say yes to pain it is going to take over your world completely. But in saying yes we are not condoning it or aiding it, we are simply recognising the truth of reality as it is right now. We are getting out of the struggle-based belief that this shouldn't be happening and into the flow-based perception that it is happening. Saying yes is really just being willing to experience present reality as it is, with no sugarcoating.

But what if you really can't say yes to what is happening? Maybe it feels too intense. Then simply say yes to your no. The question here is simple: Can I say yes to my experience? And if I can't say yes, can I say yes to my no? Just in this moment, can I be OK with this resistance?

You see, this is truly about letting go of outcomes. You are not aiming to get rid of the bad feelings by allowing them, or secretly hoping that if you just say yes they will go away. You are surrendering to the truth of your Now, which is that right now it is feeling uncomfortable. Discomfort is also God. Be the discomforted one for a while. The beauty is in your patience with yourself as you do this. The light is shining as you, even though all you see is darkness. You demonstrate the spirit of Christ Consciousness when you sit with yourself in the darkness and stay put while this energy cooks you. We are not trying to get you anywhere or change anything – change is not your responsibility. Your responsibility is Presence. Become the one who contains light and dark, and change will flow by itself.

One main effect of this practice of allowing present experience is to enable the story, the drama, to settle. In this phase we are noticing there is a story happening and that a part of us is buying into it. If we try to fix the problem we are buying into the story of a problem. So stopping, noticing and allowing is about dropping through the mental story into the pure feeling and sensation of this moment. It involves a deep welcoming of all aspects of ourselves, and this welcoming opens the door to the ease and peace we have been longing for.

Step 3: Shift into Presence

In this step we continue noticing and experiencing without judgement. And as we do that, we tune into what else is happening in our awareness. We become aware of the space in which present reality is unfolding.

So, for example, you might be experiencing a sadness or a longing for love. As you experience this while expanding your awareness you might also notice that you can hear birds singing outside and that there is a kind of stillness in the air.

So you have pain and you have stillness and a flow of current events.

After continuing experiencing and noticing for a while you might get the sense that the pain is lifting and the stillness is becoming stronger. Without you really doing anything, a shift has happened. You have gone from being fully absorbed in the experience of discomfort and lack to noticing that the Being quality of stillness is also here. You might find other qualities like joy, peace, groundedness, curiosity or strength showing up. Somehow, your simple willingness to experience your humanity has given way to your divinity. It's hard to really explain this part because it's a bit of a mystery. All I can say is that if you open-heartedly feel what wants to be felt and experienced, while maintaining a state of open awareness, at some point the pain and lack give way to fullness and the awareness of Presence. The key is your willingness to experience present reality while also observing it without judgement.

Once you are aware of the first subtle qualities of Being that appear you apply your attention to them and allow them to become more clear. So let's say that in addition to a deep stillness you are also in touch with a kind of light, playful energy. You tune into this playful energy, noticing where it appears in your field of awareness, following its movement. For instance, does it want to expand, does it want to fly, does it want to play? You just flow with it for a while, but taking care not to go unconscious and get lost in a story about it. You are remaining alert and awake, tuning more and more into whatever essence qualities appear. Playfulness might turn into compassion or into groundedness or even into ruthless truth. These are the different faces with which Being meets you. The more you tune into and recognise these causeless qualities, the more you get a sense of yourself existing as pure Presence.

Right, so now we are feeling immersed in Being and Presence. What next?

Step 4: Open to action

From our state of rootedness in Being, we turn our attention back to that problem or question we had when we entered the process and we ask a simple question: What wants to happen now? Or we can simply notice how we feel about the issue and see if a more helpful attitude comes to us. It's important here that you don't force an answer but that you simply observe your situation from the place of Being and Presence. Allow the universe, Life, to flow through you into action or into a more beneficial attitude. For example, if you were worrying about a relationship breakup, you might get the knowing that you are OK and are worthy and lovable as you are. As you flow back into the world with this knowing you will find yourself taking different actions and relating to the situation with more harmony and ease.

The whole of the above process can be shortened to this:

1. Stop
2. Allow
3. Be
4. Act

Another very simple way of looking at this is to see it as a practice of allowing, experiencing and noticing, repeated effortlessly until a shift into Presence happens. Then it is about falling deeper into Presence and seeing what actions want to arise as expressions of Presence.

The U-model

Usually when we want to change something or create something we experience a need, a feeling of lack, and then we look around for something to fill that lack. If we feel poor we look for money, if we feel unloved we look for a partner, if our self-esteem is low we look for something that we can succeed at. We find ourselves at point A, with a need, and we want to get to point B where the need is fulfilled. You can picture this as a straight line going from left to right along the page.

A ---------------------- B

The journey from A to B is a journey in time. We don't have something now, but we hope to get it in the future.

If you resonate with Stage 1 (Victim) energy, you will spend a lot of time fruitlessly drifting around point A, trying this and that without success, until you finally submit to the lure of the couch and a pizza. Point B is never attained.

If you resonate with Stage 2 (Empowerment) you will set about creating an action plan for how you can get to point B. You'll go to coaching or read books that lay out all the steps that will get you there. If your quest is spiritual, you will pray or meditate or go on retreats and do fasts. You feel inspired by the journey to B and you are encouraged by the little victories you enjoy along the way. At last you are really making progress! What happens next for Empowerment is that you arrive at point B and celebrate mightily. For a while you enjoy stillness and a sense of achievement, and then the restlessness sets in again. Point B turns out to be another Point A, and now you have a new goal to achieve.

If you resonate with Stage 3 (Wisdom) you will have a large number of experiences of turning points A into B and you will know that all B's turn into A's. This is the point where you go into despair or into enlightenment. Nothing you do by conventional means gets you what you are really looking for. You are tired of just reaching for point B all the time. So what do you do?

Well, you read this book or attend a course on this subject and you hear about something called the U-model. The U-model says that before you try to go to B, just spend a moment getting off the timetrack completely and sink into Being. Let go all the thoughts of what you think you need or should have, and relax into the timeless presence of your true nature. Then from here, look again at the time track and see if there is something you would love to do. The work is not to get from A to B in linear time, it's to drop out of time and into Being, and then to allow Being to flow into your world as beneficial change and enlightened action. You can picture this as a U shape, with a line dropping down from point A to "Being" and then up again to point B:

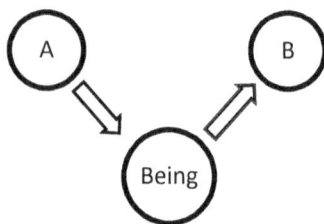

The Presence Shift process I described in the first part of this chapter follows the U-model of development. Steps 1 and 2 about stopping, noticing, and allowing are part of the downward motion towards Being. Step 3 is about accessing Being. Step 4 is about heading back up to the timeline with some actions and intentions.

I believe the U-model approach will be part of the new wave of coaching and development, and it's already finding its way into business (See Otto Scharmer's pioneering work on the U-model in corporations).

The wisdom of the U-model can be summed up in one line: First be, then do.

This book is about stopping the endless search for something that will fix us and just falling into Being, where everything we seek is already present. From the knowledge of the fullness of Being we then flow back into the world of time and space, but now our actions are aligned with Spirit or Being or Self or whatever word you use to describe the greater Life that is living through and as us. Action from here is without ego because it is a surrender to the change that is already happening.

In the conventional models of change and spiritual growth, our work is to create change and to make things happen. In the U-model approaches, our work is to recognise, support and say yes to the change that is already happening. We are the channel for that greater Life that is living us. If we think we have to create change in the world we end up at war with those who want things the way they are and we set ourselves up for failure. If we want to make change happen in ourselves, we go to war against our darker nature which wants healing and acceptance before it will move. If we try to achieve enlightenment or God consciousness or unity, all our actions merely create more distractions that keep us from the only place God could ever be, which is Now. Right here, in this messy, sticky, troublesome moment. The more we try to smooth things over and make them look like peace and grooviness, the more we avoid the true peace of Being that is already here. The steps are simple: Stop fixing, allow present experience, notice Being, then ask what wants to happen next.

The Heart-Mind Coherence technique

The Presence Shift process is a minimalistic approach that works its magic by affirming the wholeness that is already present, regardless of circumstances. It does not seek to change anything but finds the flow of wellbeing in whatever is happening in the moment. However, while it restores effortlessness to the actual process of change, it does require an exercise of will to practise it. And sometimes, because we are human, we are simply not able to maintain this very Zen-like attitude. For this reason, I am including a supplementary technique that can support our human, physical being in a compassionate way when we are feeling particularly triggered or overwhelmed.

The Institute of HeartMath has done some wonderful research into the connection between our hearts and our emotional states. Their biofeedback tools show quite clearly that what the poets have always said about the heart being the seat of love is true. When you feel low, your heart beats in an irregular pattern, and when you are feeling good it beats in a pattern that is more ordered and coherent. When the heart is experiencing love it beats in a way that promotes clear thinking and mental ease. Heart and mind become aligned in one coherent system.

HeartMath has shown that if you just take your attention off your problems and focus on the heart, while breathing in a slow and even way, the heart starts going into coherence. From here, one begins to notice naturally occurring feelings of wellbeing. If you then breathe in more of these feelings and radiate them out from the heart you create actual biochemical changes in your body that deepen the state of coherence. I use the HeartMath coherence techniques as an integral part of my coaching work. Here's my adaptation of the basic coherence practice:

1. Stop whatever you are doing to try and fix your situation.

2. Focus attention on the heart area while taking slow, deep breaths. It can help to silently count in to a count of 4 or 5 and out to the same count.

3. Notice any positive feeling in your awareness, no matter how subtle. If you can't find anything positive, simply imagine it. Fake it to make it. Breathe more of it in from the universe, and radiate it from your heart on the outbreath.

This technique is great for when you are really feeling triggered by something and your body is in a state of stress. The focusing on the heart brings the mind out of panic mode by letting it rest in one simple task. As you focus more and more on one point, you bring back the scattered thoughts that have been rushing into the past and into the future and you give them permission to rest in the non-doing of this present moment.

Paying attention to the breath and making the in-breath the same length as the out-breath restores balance to the autonomic nervous system (ANS). When we breathe in we activate the sympathetic branch of the ANS which gears us up for action, and when we breathe out we activate the parasympathetic system, which brings us into the rest-and-digest phase. Too much sympathetic activation keeps us revving in an anxious or angry state, while too much parasympathetic activation keeps us in a depressed state. So the breathing works at a very physical level to restore balance.

The third step, activating positive emotion, creates real biochemical changes that reflect and amplify the imagined positive state. By faking a good feeling you can actually create it!

On the face of it this is an inside-out approach because you are creating your own inner conditions regardless of what is happening in the outside world. However, it still has one foot in the outside-in scheme because you are still doing something to get something else. It is saying that this moment of stress is an unwanted part of the Now, which it can't be because it is already the Now.

That said, I don't see much value in trying to observe and notice your way out of a panic attack or any other strong physical state. The Buddhists have a term for techniques like this: they call it *skilful means*. Skilful means are all the techniques and processes you use that are not pure noticing but which are nonetheless supportive of noticing. The idea is that you use the skilful means practices within an overall practice of pure allowing. This prevents you from getting stuck in trying to shift all bad feelings to good ones, which is what can happen if you are using HeartMath or any other kind of tool without the deeper awareness of the perfection of the moment. Ultimately, even your fear and panic is part of the Now and so is already accepted by Life, so there's nothing you have to do about it. However, because we have compassion for ourselves, and because we know that the panic is not the whole truth of the situation, we allow ourselves the use of skilful means to restore balance. The only risk in this is when we become addicted to always being calm and feeling only good feelings. Reality will always bring us both good and bad feelings. Techniques like HeartMath coherence can help us get out of being stuck in any one of these states.

The Presence Shift and Coherence techniques can be combined in a very fluid way. They both start with stopping all our strategies aimed at fixing the situation. Then they focus on the present moment. In the presencing process we simply notice all the things that are currently appearing in awareness. In the Coherence technique, we focus on the heart area. Both of these will bring our minds out of past and future and anchor them in the present moment. From here, both approaches also look for naturally occurring positive feelings. In presencing, we identify these as qualities of Being. In the Coherence practice we are more in touch with good feelings that are physically generated by the heart as it goes into coherence. The main point of departure between the two is that in the Coherence practice it is quite acceptable to fake a good feeling in order to create the biochemical changes that make the feeling real. In the Presence practice, one would rather simply remain open to what is already here. True joy is causeless, it does not need to be generated.

Another way to understand the difference is to think of the Presence Shift as being about inquiry and "being with" pain or discomfort, while the Coherence practice is designed to shift any discomfort and attain a more coherent state. The Presence practice is about relating freely to all states, whether coherent or incoherent.

Going beyond Wisdom consciousness

This discussion about the different approaches is a good time to point out the limitations of the stage of sattva and Wisdom consciousness. In the Bhagavad Gita, Krishna is at pains to point out that the mood of sattva is not the end goal of the spiritual seeker. Each of the moods – tamas, rajas and sattva – has its limitations and ways of binding us. While sattva seems the most desirable, it binds us by fostering attachment to peace and knowledge. If we have dedicated great effort to shifting our experiences to enjoy the sattvic conditions of inner peace, wellbeing and wisdom, we will experience conflict when these conditions are disrupted. If something upsets our composure, we feel that our universe has become disordered and that this upset needs to be corrected in some way. So we meditate more or do something to restore peace. Unwittingly, we have become bound to the conditions of peace and wisdom. In other words, our joy is conditional.

Krishna tells Arjuna that his abode is beyond the three moods of nature. To join him there, you need to renounce even the attachment to sattvic peace and wisdom. Arjuna, in fretting about going to war, was attaching to harmony and assuming that his job was to create peace. Krishna tells him there is a peace that is beyond all worldly outcomes. In Chapter 2 where I described the Myth of Progress I identified this as the fourth stage of development – Unity consciousness. In Unity consciousness, war and peace are simply appearances of the One substance of all creation. The one who has attained this perspective sees rocks and dirt and gold as equal. She is not perturbed by any actions of the three moods of nature, whether they be slothful or active or peaceful. They are all simply appearances. This is what we call the realm of nondual perception. It is the true home of causeless joy.

When we perform practices that shift us from troubled states to peaceful ones, we are learning to locate the source of wellbeing within us. However, this is no more than a shifting to sattvic conditions, which – while supportive of physical and emotional health – is not the lasting peace we seek. As long as we have to do something to get something, even if that doing involves changing our feelings and emotions, we are still limited to those feelings and emotions. We are still addicted to a mood of some kind. To go beyond moods and feelings we need to step into the space of allowing all things to be as they are – including whatever disquiet and turmoil might be within us. Only when we can be at peace with our states of conflict and disquiet can we really be at peace. You see, if all we are doing is using focusing and imagination to create physiological conditions of peace, we are always going to have to keep at it. We will be on a treadmill again, constantly trying to turn negatives into positives. There is lots of value to be obtained this way, but if that's all we're doing we are going to end up exhausted. At some point we have to make peace with the war in our nature that is inevitable, given our humanity. The moods of nature will always be acting in their various ways, generating laziness, action, craving, despair, peace and wisdom. Our work is not to hold onto some of these, it is to transcend all of them.

At the end of the Gita, Arjuna goes into battle in a state of inner surrender. He has given up trying to make peace and avoid the fight. He knows that this whole event has been created by the moods of nature and that he is not attached to any outcome, whether for war or for peace. This is the peace and joy we are aiming for – not the limited peace of sattva, which is dependent on peaceful outcomes, but the peace that contains all war and suffering. This is attainable by anybody right here in this moment.

But because we are human and are at varying stages of understanding, I always counsel that we meet ourselves where we are. Sometimes, just observing and being very Zen about what's happening in our experience can be more of a challenge than we can handle, especially if we are not working with a coaching partner who can hold the space. Then I would advise that you use the approach that most resonates with you in the moment. For instance, sometimes when I feel triggered by something I simply sit with it and work with the Presence practice. But sometimes, I get the impulse to shift my state of being, so I do some breath work and focusing to access more empowered states. There is no rule about what to do if you are aware of why you are doing it. Sometimes we want to go into pure Being and experience complete peace with whatever afflictive condition is currently in our experience. And sometimes it feels better just to shift it and get some positive feeling going. Meet yourself where you are and allow the infinite intelligence of your essential being to show you what it wants to do.

Obstacles to accessing Being

If Being is our natural state, our natural Self, it should be easy to access it, right? In theory yes, but in practice it's often not the case. We need to remember that the reason we don't live in Being now is because at some stage in our development we left the state of Being and entered the world of time and illusion. Why did we do this? Quite simply, because we suffered a wounding.

No matter how good your childhood was, there would have been numerous occasions where you learnt that your natural expression was unwelcome or undesirable. For instance, maybe you drew a lovely technicolour work of art on the walls of your parents' rented apartment, just before the landlord appeared for an inspection. Your stressed-out parents couldn't help making a fuss about the disaster you had caused. Even though they loved you, you received a powerful rebuke to your natural creativity and abundance of expression. To survive, you had to take sides with your parents and discipline yourself to never ever do that again. So now you are wondering why you are creatively blocked or you feel that something terrible will happen if you display the fruits of your creative labours. And that's just from having a great childhood! If you had a difficult childhood, you will probably have a good few scars from where you had to bury a part of yourself because it was not safe to be you. Your very being was what got you into trouble, so to survive you had to cut yourself off from yourself. What a conflict! And now you want to reconnect with Being and discover the magnificence of yourself exactly as you are. Can you see why your mind might come up with some good reasons for why you shouldn't be doing this?

In the rest of this chapter I will outline some of the beliefs and experiences we put in place to keep us away from discovering our true nature.

"I get bored or afraid!"

The inner resistance to Being will appear in the guise of a rational argument telling you not to bother with this investigation, or it will come up as a feeling of discomfort. A very common one is the feeling of a void or emptiness. The emptiness is a sign you are on the right track and are leaving the mind-made reality where your problems live. To keep you away, your mind will tell you all sorts of terrible things about this emptiness and might even invoke the fear of death. Or it will make you really bored. Boredom is a great sign that you are onto something important, so don't give up. The trick is to just observe the boredom or emptiness or whatever other sensation arises. View these sensations as the guard dogs that you installed at the entrance to your being a long time ago to keep you away because it was so unsafe. But that was a long time ago and it is safe now. You have to enter the darkness of the resistance in order to get through to the light.

Most people turn away because they think the darkness and emptiness and boredom are telling them they are on the wrong track, but if you are experiencing these then you are certainly on the right track. Even if you are beset by feelings of groundlessness, as if you are slipping off the edge of a cliff, just remember that even groundlessness is appearing in a ground of something. The ground that contains groundlessness is you. You are that in which fullness and emptiness appear. Don't let either of them fool you into avoidance or craving. Keep on going, just observing and noticing and keeping faith with yourself. The more the resistance, the greater the light that awaits you.

"I just can't find the yes to what I'm experiencing!"

Step 2 in our Presence process is to allow present circumstances to be as they are. This means finding the "yes" to whatever is happening, no matter how unpleasant it is. And here is where we can encounter another block.

Firstly, our minds can tell us that if we say yes to what is happening we won't have the will to change it. For example, if you are worrying about money, your mind will tell you that if you say yes to your current situation of being penniless, you will stay that way forever. But here's what you've got to remember – by saying yes to it you are not giving it permission to stay unchanged, you're just saying that right now, this is how reality is showing up and that, just for this moment, you are not going to struggle with it. Struggle achieves nothing. The power to shift the situation comes when you stop struggling and allow the power of Being to lighten things. Saying yes is recognising that whatever is appearing is already accepted into reality and is therefore also Life. Saying yes is not about liking it or agreeing to live with it forever, it's just recognising the facts of reality as they stand.

The reality is that sometimes we are so powerfully triggered by a situation that we just cannot find any allowing or accepting. If this happens, then forget about trying to notice essence for a while and simply work with noticing the triggered state. Staying put in this part of the process is not a failure, it's a huge success that requires incredible courage and presence. Our instincts and our conditioning tells us to keep resisting our problems and trying to fix them, so just finding some kind of peace with the problem as it is can be a huge victory. Remember, this work is inquiry – it's not a solutions-based technique that needs any particular outcome. The important thing is that you sit compassionately with yourself as you go through whatever trial is visiting you. Allow the pain, the misunderstanding, the anger, the powerlessness. All of it is happening within a ground of Being. You don't have to fight your emotions because you can never be found in any emotion, no matter how uplifting. You are that which contains and takes the shape of all emotions. Finding the space of allowing is about stepping back into the recognition of your original wholeness, no matter what seems to be broken.

"I feel Presence but I don't get any answers!"

Another block can come up when you flow into the action phase and ask what wants to happen next or what you would love to do. Often, the impulse is subtle and the action is not as dramatic as you had hoped. For example, you might find that what wants to happen next is for you to simply continue sitting in this place of stillness. Your mind will yell that you have to get up and do something or else you won't have a roof over your head, but your being is content to sit for a while longer. It does take something of a leap of faith to follow the heart. And yet, when we honour this impulse, it leads to the right action that brings us what we truly need.

What I've discovered is that sometimes what wants to happen is simply that we sit and allow ourselves to be cooked by Spirit. It's like there's some kind of alchemy underway and I just have to remain in the crucible while all this ugly stuff starts boiling up. The path I am outlining in this book is not about candyfloss and unicorns, it's about the dirty work of encountering one's shadow and surrendering to all that one has been trying to avoid. So if you feel like you're being cooked or barbecued or minced or pulverised, then you are on the right track. Keep going.

"I'm afraid that if I allow things I'll become a slacker!"

This morning I worked with a client who sincerely believed she was a failure. None of my strategies for encouraging a shift in perception were working, and no matter what I said she always returned to the position that she was fundamentally wrong. I was suggesting that a more compassionate self-belief

77

might be helpful when she blurted out the real reason for resisting this: "If I soften my attitude I will become a slob and I'll never achieve what I want!"

As she said that, I recognised in my own life how powerfully that belief would sometimes arise – that if I just cut myself some slack I would become a slacker who never did anything and never achieved any kind of success. The very terms "cut myself some slack" and others like "let myself off the hook" seem redolent with failure and weakness. It seems impossible that we can actually allow ourselves to soften and be acceptable as we are.

I think this is taboo against finding satisfaction in ourselves exactly as we are is the major obstacle to realising what we most truly want. And here's why we have such a block against it: We are afraid that if we forgive ourselves and get off the treadmill of never-ending improvement we will slip back into the sloth and victimhood of tamasic consciousness. At this point in our evolution we most probably have encountered only two options, the tamasic defeatedness of "I can't" and the rajasic vigour of "I can". When we discovered Empowerment it was infinitely better than Victimhood, and the way that we elevated ourselves into that consciousness was by believing that we could change ourselves and our world. The belief in the necessity of change and the rigorous self-discipline needed to create this change is embedded in rajasic consciousness.

When we are in the Empowerment stage, our only other reference is Victimhood, so now we interpret all relaxation and ease and effortlessness as slacking. What we are not seeing is that there are further stages of development in which the whole notion of slacking is seen differently. Remember the motto of sattva? "I can't." It is exactly the same as the motto for tamas, except that it means something vastly different. The "I can't" of sattva is a powerful relinquishing of the small self for the greater Self or Life that is living through us and as us. It is a relaxing into Being, not a slacking into the comforting arms of the sofa and a sixpack of beers. However, unless we have introduced the mind to sattvic consciousness it will continue to interpret all relaxation as a regression into tamasic sloth and ignorance.

So now, when you encounter inner resistance to letting go into Being, it might be helpful to remind yourself that your surrender is actually a very active, aware and courageous undertaking and is not in any way related to the defeatism of Victim consciousness. When you make peace with yourself and with your faults, you are not giving in to them, you are accessing the power of compassion and the wisdom of Being. From a state of surrendered Being, you will find that you have more energy because you no longer have to prove yourself and constantly try to fill your inner voids with achievements. You will know that you are enough as you are, and from this place of enough, empowered actions and inspired wisdom will flow.

"I'm afraid that if I feel my true emotions I'll become depressed

A common fear that comes up when we talk about feeling the underlying pain is that we will fall back into the depression or negativity we have been trying so hard to get out of. Surely, when we were depressed, we were feeling our negativity – and look where that got us!

So here's why this is different.

When we were depressed or wallowing around in negativity we weren't actually feeling the core pain. We were feeling suppressed rage at the world or disappointment with ourselves or weariness with years of wasted effort. When we look closely, we see that these are all reactions to the original pain, not the pain itself. They are actually attacks against ourselves. What causes the hurt are the thoughts that occupy our minds like, "Why can't I get it right?", "I've worked so hard and still I'm getting nowhere", "When will God listen to me?" The depression is coming from our belief that we are at fault rather than from the original pain of having lost a quality of our inner Being or essence. The original pain is simply pain, often expressed as a deep longing. This is what I am referring to when I say that the path is through the pain. First we have to encounter the pain of our resistance and let that go, and then we get to the original pain which is always about the loss of essence. When we stay with that pain, we drop through into the fullness of that quality, which we discover is not missing after all.

The original pain is always the loss of a quality of Being, for example the loss of value or strength. In my own life I have spent years in a very depressed state which I always thought was about my frustration at not being able to find supportive work that honoured my talents and paid enough for me to enjoy a good living. But when I look at those issues now I see that the suffering was caused by me taking these losses personally. I felt I was doing something wrong or not getting it right. I flailed about, trying to bail out a sinking ship, but nothing helped. However, when I took the personal out of it I was left with the more pure pain of longing for value and creativity. What I needed to do was stop trying to find the next thing that would solve my problems and just get real with the original longing for wealth, self-expression and ease. These longings were painful in themselves, but they did not involve suffering. The suffering that drove the depression was the feeling there was something wrong with me and that what was happening shouldn't have been happening.

What I have learnt now is that when I have an attack of missing essence, my path is not to find something that will fill it but rather to sit with the original pain of loss and just to exist compassionately with it for a while. I enter the mystery of this loss, knowing that even though it is painful, there is nothing wrong with the situation or with me. I breathe in this loss, making space for it, listening to it. I let it bite. I know that if I am missing something it must already be within me somewhere. If I am feeling poor, then great wealth is calling to me. This is the spirit of the Emergence model. That which seems missing is that which you already are. And the way to discover that is to go into the pain of what seems missing. After a while of sitting with this, something usually shifts. One begins to notice the noticing space itself. When we pay attention to what else is in our field of perception we begin to notice things like compassion, stillness, power, and value.

If you are feeling unloved, the solution is not to go out and find a partner who will finally love you the way you expect to be loved. It is to go into the pain of your loss of essence and let it guide you to the love that you already are. The same goes for feeling poor or powerless or any other state. The goal of your life is not to amass fortune in the world, it is to discover it already within you. All forms of worldly success will eventually leave you feeling empty and alone if they are achieved through trying to fill a lack in yourself. Remember the Great Betrayal? Your worldly and spiritual plans will always betray you until you get it that what you are seeking is already within you. When you have found it within you, then your outer reality is free to shift to reflect this inner state of having and you end up creating and enjoying what is most beneficial to you and the world.

"But I thought the Now was supposed to feel groovy!"

A major block we can have to accessing essence and the Now is the belief that current pain or discomfort prove we are not in the Now.

Few teachers in the modern era have done more to publicise and illuminate the power of "Now" consciousness than Eckhart Tolle. He reminds us that when we let go of the stories of how things should be and just stay with the way they are, we experience deep peace and effortless wellbeing. When I first read this material I knew that I had found my true philosophy, even though at the time I felt about a million miles from the Now. Nonetheless, I set about practising awareness and making an effort to be more in the moment. And with that I fell headfirst into a huge spiritual trap.

You see, when we read people like Eckhart Tolle who have awakened deeply to the present moment we can easily assume that the apparent bliss and ease they are experiencing is a mark of them having accessed this mysterious place called the Now. We think that when we so often feel uncomfortable, disgruntled, irritated, sad or angry that we have lost the Now because, well, Eckhart Tolle never feels irritated, sad and depressed. This is the trap – the assumption that the Now includes only blissful feelings and peaceful emotions.

We read in such writers that our suffering is caused by our fear of the future or our regret over our past – and they are right. But here's the thing – even suffering is an appearance in the Now. For some of us, the woundings we have experienced might be so deep that they take a while to clear. Does that mean we are to be excluded from the Now? No, it simply means that we are called to recognise that this Now includes our suffering as part of its perfection. The lock that keeps the door of this trap closed on us is the belief that we have to shift how we feel in order to get free. In other words, we believe that we have to feel groovy like Eckhart Tolle in order to experience the Now he is telling us about. Innocently, we assume that our bad feelings are saying that we are doing something wrong and that we have lost the Now. In one sense there is truth in it, in that negative feelings point to some part of us that is not partaking of the whole truth, but it is not true of the whole of us, which is always already enlightened and a fully perfect expression of this Now.

I'm sure Tolle would agree with this, and if you read carefully you will see he is at pains to point out the trap, but we fall into it anyway. Really get this – you do not access the Now by manipulating your inner states so that you experience only comfortable or blissful feelings; you realise the Now by witnessing everything that arises right now and by simply not judging it. If pain, regret, fear or boredom are part of your reality, then they are an equal part of the whole of Life and you do not need to ignore, repress or expel them. Simply notice, allow, and open to current experience.

The instruction for recognising the Now is simple: Stop fighting the dark, then expand your awareness so that it includes not only the bright and shiny stuff but also the messy, dark and dangerous stuff. Stop looking to have only unicorns in your paradise and welcome also the tigers and scorpions. You are that which contains all forms and is all forms. The Now is God's view as he/she/it surveys the world with all its creatures and knows that each has its place and all is good.

5. LIVING THE NEW PARADIGM

The result of the Presence practice outlined in the previous chapter is to bring you in touch with the wellbeing and joy you already are, regardless of what is happening in the outside world or in the world of your thoughts and feelings. When you are in touch with Being, the realm of causeless joy, you are truly at the centre of yourself, radiating outward. Now life is no longer about trying to achieve something out there to give you a desired state in here, it is about the unfolding of that which you already are. Your work is not to make things happen but to connect with the inner conditions that support the unfolding of that which is most beneficial to you. Remember the analogy of the acorn? The acorn does not need to make itself into an oak tree – it simply needs the right conditions of earth, moisture and sunlight. If these are in place, the rest happens by itself. The immortal pattern of the acorn is activated and its destiny unfolds by itself. The acorn is doing nothing – Life is doing everything.

This is what Christ was pointing to when he spoke about the lilies of the field not having to work at being fulfilled:

Consider the lilies of the field; they neither toil nor spin, yet even Solomon in all his glory was not clothed like one of these. (Matt 6:28)

He is pointing to that in you which is already utterly accomplished and which needs no work in order to be realised. The glory you seek is already here. All that is required is that you recognise it.

The rest of this chapter discusses some questions that arise from this new way of looking at the world so that you can strengthen your understanding of the paradigm and begin applying it in your life.

The role of action

Let's begin by addressing the role of action, because although I have just been talking about the lilies of the field not having to toil, it's not so easy to apply this directly to us humans. We are more complex than plants and animals and our nature includes the realm of action and doing. As long as plants have the right conditions of soil and water and sunlight, their divine nature will do their growing for them. There's literally nothing they have to do. But if we dig a hole in the ground and stand in it and pretend to be a tree, we'll fail to thrive. In fact, we'll end up dead. Our human nature includes not only the realm of Being but also the realm of doing. So what's the relationship between them?

In previous eras, action has been necessary as a tool of survival. It has brought us towards food and shelter and away from predators and enemies. Action is what enabled us to evolve from animals. But it's fairly clear just from looking at the world that this model of survival-based action is capable of destroying us. Action done to achieve something that's not already within us will continue to generate a sense of emptiness, which prompts more action. We have become addicted to action as the only way forward. But it's not sustainable.

In the new era that is being born, action is being seen as a reflection and confirmation of an already-existing state of being. We adopt the inward state of the acorn and the lily, knowing that who we are is enough, that we have enough and that nothing can add or detract from our splendour. And from this understanding, we ask what wants to happen. What action will realise this fullness that we already are? What relationship will reflect the love I already have for myself? This is action devoid of need and arising from the fullness of causeless joy.

For example, right now I am contemplating joining a certain business networking organisation. I find myself somewhat hesitant because it requires a fair commitment of time. Part of me is saying that I should do it because it will enable me to get more clients for my coaching business. This, after all, is the stated goal of joining such an organisation – to increase business. But I also know that if I join with that attitude it is unlikely to be the success I imagine. I will be doing something to get something, essentially making a purchase by expending effort to acquire something that I don't have right now. If the purchase doesn't work out the way I hope, I will be disappointed and consider it a bad deal. So this way of thinking is not inspiring me. I recognise some desperation in it.

What's a better way?

Well, as I inquire deeper into this question now I am remembering the visit I had with the networking group and I connect with the fact that I enjoyed the experience. Everyone seemed to be looking out for one another, and there was a genuine feeling of sharing. I realise that I would love to help others be a business success, and I would certainly value learning from them. The key for me is whether I can enjoy being a member even if I don't get much extra business through them. Will my membership give me something that is beyond the stated outcome and be realisable now, without any extra business? Essentially, will my presence there be a reflection of something already within me, or will I have to have some outcome to justify my involvement? For now, I am meditating on how I might be a part of that group as a reflection of my already-existing success, friendliness and cooperative nature.

To realise the wisdom of the lilies of the field, first connect with the state of perfection that those lilies represent. Who you are requires no effort. No toiling or spinning is required. When you know this, and when you step into the rich soil of your inner being, that which Life is most inspired to create in you will be able to take root and flourish. Your primary action is to recognise and build trust in your inner worthiness. You are like the gardener who prepares the soil and then plants a seed. Your actions from there onward are not to make the seed grow but simply to keep tending the soil and ensuring the conditions remain favourable to growth. As the gardener trusts in Life, and the green shoots trust in the sun, so too are we called to trust in that which is living as us and through us. Let action follow surrender to this greater intelligence, not stand in opposition to it. The right place for action is after the surrender to this life force, not before it. This is the way of non-action – action without attachment to outcome. And this non-attachment to outcome is the mark of one who lives from the mood of sattva, or surrender.

Enlightened manifestation

A lot has been written on the use of intention and the Law of Attraction to create wealth and to fulfil your desires. From this perspective, manifestation is all about doing something or changing something in order to get something else. However, from the perspective of this book, if you are using laws of the universe to attract things to you, then you are starting from a place of separation and so will continue to attract separation into your life. This is not to say that the Law of Attraction is wrong, for a law of the universe can never be wrong. It's just saying that if you are using a tool to get something that's not here right now, your creation will be based on the absence of that which you most desire. In other words, what you create will bring you happiness for a while, but it will not feed your soul. The only thing that can feed the soul is the soul itself. Enlightened manifestation begins with the realisation that nothing is ever missing and that you do not actually need anything (though you might love to experience certain things).

But what about our desires? Aren't we meant to fulfil them?

We have misunderstood what desires are and how they should be fulfilled. In the outside-in model, a desire is something you want – something you don't have now but which you have a strong urge to get. Your wants are seen as things that are missing from your life. So if you are a student of the Law of Attraction, you might start intending and visualising and doing things that align you with the vibration of the desired object. Nothing wrong with that – it's just that what you desire is usually not what you really want.

What you really want is to rest in the knowledge that you are already everything you seek. You access this knowledge when you view the world through the lens of the Emergence model. Under this model, our needs point not to what we are lacking but to something that we already are that wants to emerge. Any effort to create something that satisfies a lack will fail to satisfy because it hasn't touched the deeper truth of our original fullness. So in the Emergence model, a desire is an invitation to inquire into what we already are. Our needs are first experienced as holes or absences, but when we simply stay with those sensations of absence rather than reaching for some or other substance to fill them we will arrive at the realisation of original fullness. Our needs are glaring reminders of what we already have but are simply not recognising.

For example, suppose you have been single for a long while and you feel that you really need a partner. You experience a deep need for someone to complete you. Perhaps you have been reading books on how to call in the man or woman of your dreams. You are following every self-improvement and Empowerment consciousness strategy you can find to make yourself attractive to others and to resolve your relationship issues. But still ... nothing.

You begin to feel down because you have put in all this work and you are still single. Why has the Law of Attraction not worked?

Or perhaps you have indeed attracted a partner and now you are happy. But what happens if this partner turns out to be not so nice after all? What happens if they leave you or you leave them? Will you still be happy?

You see, when you follow this line of approach to manifesting your desires you are pandering to the surface level of the desire and are filling it with substitutes. You are medicating it with substances, just like any drug user. If you get a partner under these conditions you will still not have solved the original problem of your aloneness. If you think you need a partner to complete you, you will never be complete. The Great Betrayal will eventually awaken you to the fact that you need nobody. Of course, relationships are enriching and very nice to have, but they are not a solution to any problem. In the era of survival they were a solution to the survival of the tribe, but unless that dynamic still has meaning for you then you are better served by looking elsewhere for true fulfilment.

What you are really looking for is not a partner but rather the essence quality of love that is already your true nature. You have simply become estranged from it and are now projecting it as the need for another person.

So let's say you are experiencing the need for a relationship. You recognise that no person will ever truly satisfy you, so you decide to do some inquiry on this need. You feel into the need and you experience all its nuances. For example, you may feel a sort of tugging in the heart, or perhaps a coldness in the belly. You feel all of it and you allow it. You find the yes to current experience. Right now, you are experiencing the empty side of the universe. You avoid rushing out to fill it with something, because you know that will only be a substitute, a drug. As you sit with the expression of this need and desire without buying into its story, the story begins to settle. In the stillness that follows you become aware of that which surrounds the desire. The emptiness and lack are taking place within a fullness. You notice the particular flavours of this fullness. Perhaps light and playful, perhaps deep and serious, perhaps loving and compassionate. You enjoy this play of lack and fullness, while putting more and more attention on the fullness.

When you feel well grounded in the fullness of Being, you look at your question on relationships and see how it appears from this perspective. Do you still *need* someone, or would you simply *love* to have someone so that you might enact and experience the love that is already your true nature? The energy of need will always create more neediness, but the energy of having and wanting to share creates more having and sharing. When you no longer need a partner, the right partner has a good chance of showing up. But once again, don't go attaching conditions to it. Sometimes you get a partner, sometimes you don't. The material fulfilment of the desire is not up to you.

The same goes for any other creation you would love to bring into this world. First, treat the desire and the longing as indication of what you already are. Find the fulfilment of this within you. Then, from that space of fulfilment, ask what wants to happen and follow through with those actions.

Visualisation and visioning

Do you remember our discussion of visualisation vs. visioning in Chapter 3? Visualisation is an Empowerment strategy to create what seems to be missing. It stays within the known world and the realm of the ego and tries to rearrange the components to bring you what you think you need. Visioning, on the other hand, let's go of all desire and goes into the unknown of perfect stillness. In the place beyond desire, all that you desire is already met. From this place, that which you are but which you are not yet recognising is free to emerge into the manifest world. When you Vision, be prepared for answers that don't fit what you expected. For instance, if you visualise a desired partner, you will imagine all their good qualities and how it will be to spend time with them. However, when you vision, you let all that go and you dwell in the essence qualities of having and loving. Then you ask what is the highest expression of that essence that wants to manifest in your life. The answer might not be a new romantic partner. It might be a holiday, or a new job, or nothing new – just the realisation that you are splendid exactly the way you are.

Can one combine visualisation and visioning?

Yes indeed. Visualisation can be the booster rocket for visioning. For instance, suppose you want to manifest a new car. You start by doing your visualising work and all those nice Law of Attraction techniques you learned. Perhaps you create a vision board or get a computer screensaver with a stunning picture of your car. Now if this is the highest wisdom you know, then you'll continue doing your visualisation until you reach the resonance of that new car and you attract (hopefully!) it into your life. But if you're wise to the limitation of this approach, you'll want to go further and access the field of limitless possibilities where you allow creation to happen *for* you.

So here's what you do. You've already gotten all excited and fired up by your visualisation work. You really feel that it's now possible to get this car. But instead of going out and buying it, you go into visioning. From this state of positive expectation and excitement created by visualisation, you go into surrender mode by asking a question: God, Universe, Self – what do I really want to do? What is the highest and most beneficial expression of my self that now wants to emerge into my world?

And then you hang out in the stillness for a while and see what answer comes to you. Perhaps it will be to buy that car; perhaps not. Listen for the desire that is beneath the desire for the car. Is it the feeling of success, the feeling of having arrived? Is it the feeling of celebration as you attain a desired outcome? These are all qualities that are already part of your true nature and do not need the possession of a new car in order to be realised. When you connect with these qualities, whatever you create will be created by Life itself. You are merely the channel through which that life enters the world of form.

Enlightened manifestation is about visioning – it is about entering the not-knowing space of true Being and letting it fill the voids that have appeared in your life.

The enlightened use of the Law of Attraction is to first take care of the vibration you are offering, making sure you are vibrating at the frequency of Being rather than of lack. Now from here, you flow into what wants to happen in your life and you take the actions that feel the most inspired or helpful. The enlightened manifester combines the "I can" of Empowerment with the divine "I can't" of Wisdom, knowing that anything is possible but that he or she is not in control of the outcome. It is good to work on your money and relationship issues and clear your negative beliefs, but let these endeavours be conducted within the deeper knowledge that you are already a perfect expression of the One, even with your faults in place. After working on your limiting beliefs, sit back for a while and notice those beliefs that remain and just become present to the divine play that is happening through you and as you. There is something of a paradox here – that you work at changing your expression, even while knowing you are divine exactly as you are. Being does not see this as a contradiction but rather as part of the game of Spirit in the world. Remember, your goal is not to exclude aspects of reality but to include and transcend. You include the "I can" of rajas as you embrace the "I can't" of sattva. They are not contradictory when viewed through the eyes of wisdom.

I am aware that in this book I have taken a critical approach to the Law of Attraction, but this is really just a reaction against the common interpretation of it as a means to get something and as a covert method of controlling outcomes and avoiding pain. Do not let this limit your explorations of the subject, for there are different levels of understanding for all concepts and models. The point I am wanting to get across in this book is this – that you have attained to mastery not when you can create whatever your heart desires but when you find your heart's desire in everything that appears. This is the ultimate surrender and the ultimate freedom. Once you have tasted this freedom, then you can have fun with manifestation processes because you are not acting from neediness but from fullness. The universe's desire for expansion and for the expression of joy unencumbered by expectations is then free to express itself through you. Now you are a channel for the divine. Your desires are aligned with the desires of the universe. You want what Life wants. And that is true peace.

Your true calling

Imagine for a moment that you are a life coach for animals and creepy crawlies. One day, a lovely, hairy caterpillar comes to your office looking a bit stressed and forlorn. As a good coach, you ask what's bothering Ms Caterpillar and begin to inquire into her life goals. She confesses she has been a high-achiever caterpillar – an A-type caterpillar – and has worked her way up the caterpillar ladder to be one of the foremost caterpillars of the forest. She had her sights set on even greater achievements, but lately she has been feeling really demotivated. The things that used to inspire and excite her no longer do. She's fallen into a rut. Even her appetite seems to have disappeared! If she's really truthful, she confesses, she's begun to lose all interest in being a caterpillar and has this huge urge to just spin a cocoon and lie there for a while and do nothing.

So here's the question: Do you, as the foremost life coach of the forest, continue trying to coach Ms Caterpillar on how to get her caterpillar mojo back? Or do you subtly suggest that this rut she's fallen into might not be such a bad thing after all?

The caterpillar's calling is the dissolution of the caterpillar and the emergence of something the caterpillar cannot imagine. In the same way, your calling is that which is seeking to emerge through you right now and which might in some way be troubling to the ego self. A true calling comes from beyond the little you – it is Life, seeking to express itself in matter. Consider the careers that are often described as involving a calling – teaching, nursing, being an artist or writer, and serving as a priest or pastor. These are not glamorous jobs and they usually involve hard work without much financial reward. If you follow these kinds of career paths you are doing it for love rather than money and because you are answering the call of your heart. And yes, you can have a calling to be a great businessperson and make lots of money, but if it is a true calling that business will probably be more about changing people's lives than about pure profit.

People who follow a calling are following an inner light and their actions are in service to a greater good. Working for the greater good might sound wonderful, but it can present severe challenges in day to day life. Think of artists labouring away for years to perfect their craft and create meaningful works of art. Many of them have a hard life in terms of material wellbeing and even psychological health. In traditional societies, shamans and healers are called by the gods or the ancestors and often undergo severe trials in order to access their gifts of Spirit. Healers, shamans, mystics, artists and others who are born to a calling often find themselves on the fringes of the society they long to serve. The calling comes from beyond the little self, and as such can be threatening to the little self and its ego desires. This is why we often end up avoiding our calling.

And yes, everyone has a calling of some kind. Not all are dramatic and all-encompassing. Some are very simple. For instance, the awakening of spiritual interest is a calling that comes from beyond the ego. For some, just following that calling in a small way – for instance by reading certain kinds of books – is enough to get them into trouble with their community. The calling is not interested in your success as a personality, it is interested in your transformation.

Something is whispering in my ear right now that I must say something about mothers and parents in general. Yes, being a parent is also a calling, if you enter into it as a service, as a calling of love. You sacrifice some of your ambitions for the good of the child and the family as a whole. The ego would never do this, but Life would. If you are a mother or father who is perhaps feeling burdened by parenthood, while at the same time quite clear that you wouldn't give it up for anything, you are following a calling. It is perhaps not a calling of a lifetime, but it is a calling of now. It is your spiritual path for this part of your life. Nobody would consciously choose to be woken up every two hours through the night to care for a baby, and yet a loving parent is willing to do it. This is the essential condition of the calling – something that the conscious, ego personality would not choose, but which some deeper part of the self is choosing. As such, the calling is always transformative because it involves the sacrifice of the personal will for the greater will of Life.

In light of this, we all have a calling. For most of us it is not something grand, it is simply the moment by moment impulse of Life to experience itself in a certain way. Following your calling means tuning in to what wants to happen now, rather than trying to plan everything and get things organised just the way you like it. Your life is not a journey from A to Z, it is an unfolding of the timeless Now. The calling is the unfolding. You don't always know where it is going, you just know that something is impulsing you to do something. This is what it means to live from the Emergence model, trusting that Life knows where you are going, even when your conscious mind does not. An essential skill of living the Emergence way is to tolerate not-knowing. When following the calling of the moment in the unfolding Now, you will usually only see one step ahead of you. You only know what is right for this moment. And sometimes that can be challenging. If you don't have money for rent and your impulse in this moment is to relax further into Being, the ego mind will resist. You will experience discomfort and alarm. The calling is not concerned about your ego needs; it wants only one thing – to experience an aspect of the divine in the world. When you follow this impulse, you will be guided by the bounty of Life itself, but perhaps not always in a way that meets the rather narrow standards of your ego. Following your calling and living your essence can require the sacrifice of those ambitions that are not in alignment with the greater unfolding of Life that is living through you and as you. I am saying this here so that you are not caught unawares when the challenges arise. I am also saying it so that if you are currently being challenged you might find new meaning in the challenge that will give you hope. Is this really something bad that is happening, or is it simply the confounding of your caterpillar ambitions so that a greatness you cannot yet imagine may be born?

Getting therapy or coaching

As someone who is drawn to discovering the source of causeless joy, you will probably also be drawn to practices of self-realization and transformation. However, there is an irony here in the fact that any practice that promises some gain in the future is only going to take you away from the bliss that exists right now as your true nature. Any form of doing something to get something else is an avoidance of what is already here.

That said, it would be playing into the duality trap to declare all practices invalid. Saying there's nothing you can do to achieve enlightenment is a truth, and yet the moment we make it a belief or a rule it becomes just one more limiting fixation. I am more interested in the possibilities for practice and work within the overall understanding that nothing has to be done. The Zen-Buddhists are well aware of the contradictory nature of practice and enlightenment, saying you can't practise or meditate to find something that you already are. However, if you don't work and practise at it, you won't perceive who you are. They solve this dilemma by saying that we meditate simply because that's what Buddhas do. We meditate not to get enlightenment but as an expression of our already-existing enlightenment. So let's adopt the same attitude to the subject of practices, therapies and coaching. Could we embark on inquiry and inner work with an attitude of expressing already-existing wholeness, rather than as an attempt to fix something that is broken?

I like to think the answer is yes.

When you are awake to your essential wholeness, you will naturally want to inquire into the parts that feel like they are not participating in wholeness. But here's the catch – you're not doing so to get them to wholeness, but to understand how they are already expressions of your wholeness. If you were not already love, you would not feel the loss of love. The loss is related to the fullness of who you already are.

For example, suppose you are feeling upset because a relationship has broken down. Suddenly all the feelings of loneliness and low self-worth that the relationship had kept at bay come flooding back. You feel yourself identifying with beliefs like "I am incapable of love" or "Why can't I get it right?"

In conventional practices we will treat this as a problem to be solved. You will be regarded as someone with issues around love and self-worth, so therapy or coaching will try to figure out how these beliefs got installed and will then try to install more empowering beliefs in their place. It will be assumed that your problem really is a problem and that you need to do something to get better.

Now let's look at it from the presupposition of original wholeness. If you come to me saying you have a problem with your relationships and are feeling all torn up because your latest one has crashed, I will not assume that anything is actually wrong. I will simply be curious about your experience in this moment. Together we will inquire into the exact feelings that are arising now as you talk about your relationship, without trying to fix anything. I have found that when someone's inner mind realises we are not trying to fix anything, it relaxes because it feels heard and accepted. Now our work is to listen to and make space for all the feelings, emotions and thoughts that want to express themselves.

I will also ask gentle questions that help you clarify what is most important for you. For example, I might say something like, "It seems this breakup is reminding you of your parents' breakup. Is that true?" This simple reflection (as opposed to analysis) gives you the experience of being heard and understood, without pushing you to change anything. And it gives you the chance to clarify whether this really is true. In clarifying, we get a sense of relief. The feeling "yes, that's it" brings a natural release of the surface aspects of the story.

When you are given the space to express everything and to explore all the aspects of your story, without the pressure to change anything, the story naturally begins to settle. At a certain point you might notice an energy shift, a moment when the story lightens and you no longer feel so driven by it. You might actually be more in contact with the original pain and be feeling it very intensely, but you will no longer be fixated as much on the outer story. For instance, you might be in touch with the pure feeling of abandonment that has been underlying your distress about the breakup. So while it might actually feel more painful at this point, there is also the feeling of "yes, this is it". At this point you are letting go of the surface story and getting more in touch with what you are really feeling. You are not angry with your partner or yourself, you are feeling abandoned. So this feeling of abandonment is the core issue. Unlike conventional approaches, we are not going to try and fix this in any way, we are going to expand our view.

At this point I will shift perspective from your story to the present moment (Step 3 of the Presence Shift process). I might invite you to tell me what is occurring in your awareness right now. For example, as you recognise this story of abandonment, what else do you notice? What is happening in your energy field? What do you feel? You will begin to tell me what you notice: birds outside, the sound of traffic, some stillness, some doubts, a feeling of sadness in the heart. As we notice these sensations without commenting on them, we drop out of the story of our lives and into the present moment .... into Being. Now, as you relate your impressions, I will listen out for statements that reflect contact with this Being or essence. For example, if you say you notice a stillness behind the sound of traffic, I might ask you to tell me more about that stillness. How deep is it, how wide, how high, is it inside or outside? In this way you begin to tune in to essence, noticing more and more of it. The essence quality might change. For example, stillness might become peace or it might become playful and childlike. Whatever essence qualities show up, we tune into them and appreciate them.

After a while, when you are feeling clearly in touch with essence, I might direct your attention back to the original situation and ask how you feel about it now. Say you are in contact with a light, playful, innocent quality of Being and I invite you to look at your breakup, you will be seeing it in a completely different light. You might become aware of some action that feels appropriate, or you might perceive a more helpful attitude to have towards it. Maybe you are not such a failure at love after all, because from this state of resting in Being you are feeling light and playful and you know that your primary relationship is always with yourself, and that you are whole and complete no matter who is in your life or who is leaving it.

In this way, we do coaching and inquiry but without seeking to change anything. The irony is that by letting go the need to change anything, inspired change is free to happen. Your natural wholeness will seek expression, and our work is simply to listen to where it wants to go.

Resolving trauma and unconscious beliefs

Sometimes, in order to reconnect with lost essence, we might want to go a bit deeper and resolve traumatic past experiences. In pure essence work we don't assume there is a first cause to any pain because that gets us into fixing mode. However, I have observed that sometimes there is an apparent first cause that presents itself to be explored. The key word here is "explored", not fixed. This is an unfolding of a repressed story so that it might be heard, acknowledged and released.

For instance, sometimes when I am working with clients they spontaneously regress to childhood traumas or even to what appear to be a past-life situations. When we explore and resolve the issues in those scenes, they experience a sudden and powerful release of emotional pain and they gain access to the qualities of Being that had been held back due to the trauma. One client I worked with recently had a problem with weight and couldn't resist taking extra portions of food. When we inquired into this she found herself spontaneously reliving an apparent past life as an impoverished Chinese peasant who died of cold and hunger. The theme of that life was, "there isn't enough food". This belief was still active in her life now and was keeping her from relaxing into the natural abundance of her inner being. This is not about believing in past lives, it's about listening to the painful stories that appear and allowing the power of Being to restore a sense of wholeness and abundance.

So if you have chronic emotional issues and suspect they might be about some unresolved past experience, I heartily recommend you seek out a good regression therapist or anyone else who can do the deep stuff. I believe that one's deepest pain holds the greatest gift. When you do this work you recover all that you thought you had lost, but you get the added gift of wisdom and freedom. When you know that you never really lost anything, you need never be fooled by loss again. This is a gift to you and the gift that you begin to share with others. Whatever you struggle with most deeply is the gift that you have come to share with the world.

Working with the dark emotions

If you've read other books about how to be happy and successful you might have been given tools that enable you to banish your feelings of fear, anger and sadness. But by now you might have discovered that while these tools might work for a while and bring some relative relief, they have not ended your suffering. Conventional self-help and coaching is all about changing negatives to positives, and while this is a step forward in the search for happiness, it never actually takes us there. As long as we are searching for something that we already have, we will never find it.

Let's take fear as an example. Fear is a product of thought. But not any thoughts – thoughts that we believe and engage in. To engage in thought is to leave the awareness of the present moment and fly into an imagined future or past. When we are rooted in the Now, in open awareness, thoughts appear but they do not get to us. We don't engage them and hitch a ride on them.

So what do most of us do when we experience fear? We realise we are thinking about something that isn't real, so we try to replace our thoughts with better ones. We are simply following the advice we've read in the self-help books about turning negative thoughts into positive ones.

And here's where we fall into a nice big trap.

If we are changing our thoughts, we might get a nice feeling and be more productive for a while, but we are still messing about with things that aren't to do with this moment of Now. As soon as you get involved in trying to change thoughts and think differently, you are engaging in thought, and this engagement takes you out of the only place you will ever truly be safe from fear. Changing your thoughts is an attempt to control the situation, and the basis of this is fear. We are using fear of fear to try and control fear. No wonder we have such disappointing results! We are going to war with ourselves so we can be at peace.

A more effective antidote to fear is to cut it off at its source – at the instant where we leave the present moment. The cure is to return to the simple, aware presence that is our true nature. We simply notice the fear or whatever other afflictive state is bothering us. But be careful – this doesn't necessarily mean we suddenly start to feel good. That is one more attachment to an outcome and one more excursion into time. It means we allow current experience to be exactly as it is, including the fear and discomfort. What then becomes apparent is that there is a place of peace and safety within you, even though the fear might still be active. The part that witnesses and is aware of the fear is the peace you are looking for. From this perspective, fear is not a problem.

Fear and other afflictive states are seen as problems when we lose ourselves in trying to fix them. But when they are seen as just expressions of reality we are not drawn out from ourselves into a battle with them. The peace of your true nature can exist quite comfortably with any discomfort. The suffering of fear, envy and depression and other dark emotions is multiplied when we believe we should banish them if we want to be whole. But we are already whole, and the uncomfortable emotions are simply sensations that arise when our awareness becomes fixated in time. Even this fixation is God and is not to be banished. Banishing just creates more rejection and more time-based consciousness. As always, the remedy is to let go into open intelligence and the realm of causeless joy. But don't go looking for joy, just relax into what is here right now, no matter how that shows up.

Sometimes what shows up is more pain. But it is pain that wants to be experienced so that it can be at rest. Ultimately, these afflictive states are simply aspects of Being that want to be experienced, and they will continue to appear no matter how much we try to repress or transcend them.

The key to your freedom is really to see the painful emotions as part of your perfection. They do not say anything about you, though they appear to. They will tell you that you are failing in some way, but the "you" they are pointing to does not exist. You are the space that both contains and comprises the light and the dark emotions. Freedom is relating in an open way to all expressions that arise in your experience, even the uncomfortable ones. We have such a stigma against feeling bad that we assume we are bad for feeling bad. But discomfort and bad feelings will always arise due to our human existence. The duality of our existence is not transcended by changing all negatives to positives, it is resolved by removing our self-identity from both positions and returning it to the non-judgemental noticing space that is aware of all conditions and is attached to none.

If you are experiencing fear or any other afflictive state right now, let's see what happens if we just allow it to be there. Let's just do nothing about it except be with it. Welcome it in. This too is God, Life. Feel the texture of it. Is it jumpy, sharp, dull, sickening, heavy? While it is true that the fear is coming from your thoughts having gone into an imagined future, it is also true that while this is happening it is part of the perfection of your life. Do not fall for the trap of thinking you have to change things to make yourself more of God than you already are. If fear, depression, envy, irritation or any other afflictive state is here, so be it. Just notice it and allow it. You might find it helpful to breathe into it. Take a slow, deep breath of it – not to get rid of it but to invite it in and make space for it. On your out breath, have a sense of physical letting go. The breathing will support your body if it is in a chemical and neurological state of agitation or depression. So you're just breathing and meeting this discomfort, demonstrating the courage and compassion of your true nature. Your work is not to escape the dark emotions, it is to go into them and be with them, shining your light, though you feel lost in darkness. Your light is measured not by how many good feelings you can collect but by how you shine when bad feelings overwhelm you. Feeling low is part of life. Your mastery is in how well you can relate positively to yourself and the world when these circumstances appear. When you can love despite being persecuted, you have entered the realm of mastery. Once again, the metaphor of the crucifixion is apt here. Your job is not to insist that you get off the cross; it's to shine the light from your cross and to see the divinity in everything just as it is. Everything is God. All of it, without exception.

6. DEEPENING INTO ONENESS

This chapter presents a series of brief essays on aspects related to the Emergence model and our journey of deepening into Being.

Magic vs. mysticism

By now you might have realised that the path being described in this book goes beyond self-empowerment to the transpersonal realm of pure Being.

The path of self-empowerment involves the use of mental and metaphysical tools to manipulate the elements to create desired effects. In older language we would call this the path of magic. The path of liberation, however, is a mystical path. It does not concern itself with manipulations of any kind. The pilgrim on the mystical path seeks only to divest herself of all the coverings that hide the true Self. The path of the magician is one of gain, while the path of the mystic is one of loss. The mystic is engaged in that alchemy that dissolves the self so that the Self beyond self can be born.

Mystics do not choose themselves; the path is too rigorous for anybody to want to follow it by choice, and the rewards are uncertain. Very few people want to let go of the powers that magical manipulation promises them. True mystics are born, just as visionary artists and social revolutionaries are born. The path is a calling, and often not a happy one, for society has not always treated its mystics well. That said, I also believe that the time has come for people to awaken in a more easy and graceful way to the truths of their transpersonal divinity. Few of us are called to go all the way through the various Dark Nights to the fully realised stage of Unity consciousness, and yet many of us are being called to engage with the mystical teachings of transformation and liberation. It is like we no longer have a choice – our myriad frustrations and failures, coupled with our deep desire for happiness, force us into states of contradiction and crisis that lead either to a hell of avoidance or to the heavenly realisation that bliss is always present as our true nature. You are the refuge you have been seeking. Once you discover this, the mystic path of renunciation and renewal opens to you.

The path of the modern mystic will for a while still be a fairly solitary one, for as a species we are still exploring the realms of Victimhood and Empowerment. Most of us have not yet exercised our powers enough to discover their limits. When the limits come, when the dream of eternal progress fades, then we get to discover the gateway of humility through which we enter into the greater life that lives through us and as us. Most of the world is not there, but if you have made it thus far then you most certainly are. We speak to one another as "you" and "I", but we are not these separate beings with defined endings and beginnings, we are the One appearing as the many. The stillness that I feel right now behind these words is the same stillness that you will feel when you pause for a moment to notice. The "I" that I take myself to be in these moments beyond language is the same I that you partake of when you are still and let the naming of things be at rest. Try telling that to your business partner or to the worthy gentlemen of your local chamber of commerce! The world at large has not much use for what we have been discussing here, and yet it is the medicine that we all crave. It is the recipe for true happiness. So let me state it again: To be happy, give up trying to arrange everything so you get your way and instead relax into the joy of your true nature. Any effort to improve things beyond a certain point merely delays the moment when you meet yourself here in the raw, unedited present. No matter what is happening in your life you can be in bliss right now, in fact you are in bliss, just not recognising it. You are placing conditions on your happiness, waiting for certain things to happen so that you can call yourself a success. You are seeking a cause for your joy, not understanding that joy is without cause. If you seek it in the world of cause and effect you will never find it. You will find its substitutes, but by now you are tired of them. You no longer fall for their glamour, or at least not for long. Cease with the searching and look for the one who is doing the searching. Let the subject find the ever-subject. You think you are searching for happiness, but there is no "you", and therefore it is happiness that is seeking happiness, God that is seeking God. Your very seeking is the body of God seeking the body of God. There is nobody else here. It's just you. No matter what you do or where you go, it's all just you. Does that make you feel alone? This is what the mystics call the flight of the Alone to the Alone. It is fullness, discovering its emptiness. The emptiness fills every inch of the cosmos in such a radical way that it can only be perceived as a fullness. Emptiness and fullness are non-separate. Let the aloneness be reborn as delight, let your divine emptiness fill every inch of the cosmos with radical presence. And do not speak of this to the neighbours lest they call the men in white coats to take you away.

"Wisdom is knowing I am nothing, love is knowing I am everything, and between the two my life moves. – Nisargadatta Maharaj

Finding peace with all emotional states

Our deeper work is not to exchange bad feelings for good ones, it's to find the centre from where we can experience the full range of human emotions without taking any of them personally. Happiness, sadness, loneliness, pleasure. These states are always in flow, and when we allow them to flow we discover the freedom of our true nature behind them. We are fond of saying things like "I'm happy" or "I'm sad", but in truth we are never any one of those states, we are that which is aware of any passing state. The moment we engage in states and try to change them we are adding more conditions to our experience, more judgement that fixates our awareness on the content of our lives and involves us in an endless quest of improvement.

If we are always resisting our inner emptiness, we will constantly be seeking ways to fill the hole in ourselves. We shop, work, take drugs or meditate. We find we are constantly doing something to avoid the black hole in the centre of our lives. Even our spiritual practices become attempts to fill the hole with something. Light, visions, affirmations ... all the well-meaning but fruitless attempts to avoid the fact that we cannot control our lives. The one we take ourselves to be is not the one who we really are. In seeking bliss we keep it ever from us. The bliss we seek is already here, in this very moment, with all our discomfort and trouble still in place.

The practice is very simple. Stop trying to get somewhere, and be here where you already are. Notice what is arising. Become aware of yourself as the witness. Relax into open awareness and the realm of causeless joy. You can be in joy right now without changing anything in your life. Feel your loneliness, your abandonment, your failure. Let it bite. As you keep faith with yourself by sitting with this feeling you have been avoiding you might begin to notice that the discomfort occurs within a space. At first the pain might seem to fill every available inch of the universe, and yet something is aware of this pain. That awareness is the spaciousness and release you are looking for. But know that there will be many inducements from the mind that keep you away from this realisation because it is not in the interests of the ego to let you discover the door to your prison. It would rather have you build another prison with a better view and give you the illusion of freedom for a while. But it will always be just one more prison. The door to your freedom is here, right now, with whatever is going on in your life. Just stop for a moment and let all effort go. Relax into Being. As you do this, you might notice the great clamour of all that seems to be wrong in your life, but you will be noticing it from a place of stillness. Could it be that this clamour, this riot of discomfort, is really non-separate from the stillness that observes? When we refrain from naming the cause of our discomfort it becomes just one more event in a canvas of neutral events. In dropping our judgements and our naming of things as good or bad we end the separation between ourselves and these occurrences. You can try it right now. Think of something you have been troubled by. Then simply stop naming and identifying the causes and effects of things.

What happens?

If you give yourself the time and space to do this, you will get a sense of how the troubling events are just occurrences that appear without cause in a neutral space of awareness. There is no you and that, just present experience.

We do not have to get rid of any emotional state, for in doing that we re-create the self that is in opposition to the undesired state. In other words, we re-create the self that is capable of suffering. However, when we allow things to be as they are we step beyond the subject-object duality that holds suffering in place. Now, pain or discomfort arise, but we do not take personal ownership of them. We do not separate ourselves out from the flow of experience. Pain and pleasure arise, and we are the bliss that encounters them. Our call is to be in this world but not of it. Being of the world means fighting for so-called good against so-called bad, and hoping that one of them will win. Being in the world but not of it means engaging in the world without expectation of an outcome because all desires are already achieved in the causeless joy of your true nature. The aim is to discover your freedom in every circumstance, no matter how dire.

Now don't imagine you are suddenly going to fall into this perception of bliss, because that is just another trap of expectation. Sometimes the Now holds experiences that don't feel like bliss at all. Sometimes we will be overwhelmed. The important thing is to have a practice of returning to open intelligence in the midst of challenge and learning to trust it. Find the knowing that all is well, even if on the surface it seems everything is going to hell.

Hopelessness as the door to freedom

There are two kinds of hopelessness. The first is the hopelessness of victimhood and the mood of tamas. This is the hopelessness that couldn't be bothered to get up off the couch because, well, what's the use anyway? In this state, we are unaware of our power to change our lives, so we go about hoping that someone else will do things for us. Our inevitable and repeated disappointment can throw us into a downward spiral of despair that can last until the end of our days. For some of us, this hopelessness deposits us in a black hole where we discover that our lives are truly in danger unless we get real about who we are and start doing things differently. For many, this is a religious experience and we say we are born again. For others, it is simply the arrival of hope. Somehow, in our darkest moment, we found the core of ourselves and experienced a turnaround. The arrival of hope is the gateway to the Empowerment phase.

The second hopelessness occurs when we have spent ages in Empowerment and have achieved all kinds of success, only to find that we are still unhappy. Still, despite all our coaching and intending and our inner work, the things that are most important to us remain beyond our reach. With a huge despondency we collapse and say, "I can't!" There is a great sense of loss and frustration in this because it seems we are returning to the powerlessness of tamas. But what we are not seeing is that this second hopelessness, just like the first, is a gateway to something we could not imagine. In this case, the hopelessness is the ego and it's "I can" attitude encountering the divine "I can't". It is something of a death experience, so no wonder it is painful!

What is dying here is the very hope that saved our lives when we were in such a bad state in tamasic victimhood. We thought hope would carry us on its uplifting wings forever, but now it has abandoned us. Can you guess why hope has to die if we are to find our true freedom?

Here's a clue: Hope is about something being better in the future.

But your freedom is in the Now. The illusion of a better future is the fuel of Empowerment, but it is useless in the realm of enlightenment. To really wake up to the dream we need to let go of the illusion of a better future. Because this is it. This moment, right now. This is God. With all your faults, failures, successes, strengths and weaknesses. There is nowhere else to be but here. Your true freedom begins when you stop chasing a better tomorrow and discover the beauty and love and power that is available for you right here and now.

Remember our earlier discussion on the obstacle being the way? Whatever is in the way, is the way. The arrival of the second hopelessness is the huge obstacle – the rock – that suddenly appears in the path and shatters the illusion of everlasting progress and achievement. We interpret it as a block, a failure, but it is really the unimaginable making its presence known. It is Life, saying it is time for us to give up our caterpillar ambitions and awaken to something of an entirely different order.

If you read the literature of spiritual awakening you will find that time and again the writers tell a story of how, in a moment of utter hopelessness, they surrender their futures to the present moment. You can read this in the accounts of Eckhart Tolle, Byron Katie, John of the Cross and numerous others. The road to freedom is not paved in gold, it has some scary death scenes in it, and you are the one who gets the chop. I am bringing this to your attention because if you don't know what's happening you can begin to feel you are doing something wrong, when in fact you are on the right track. The way to deal with the arrival of this divine hopelessness is to surrender to it. Now you can't "do" surrender, but you can at least let go your resistance to what is happening. You can stand there and say, "OK, this is feeling pretty scary, I'm really losing it here. I wonder what this is about; I am open to finding out."

If you do this with humility and an open heart you might discover that God is shouting loudly in your ear: *You are perfect and divine as you are ... let all your ambitions go .. all your hopes for tomorrow ... you are not separate from your life ... this is where your freedom begins ... this is it!*

The first hopelessness is a sign you must get off your butt and do something. The second hopelessness is a sign you must collapse in a heap and do nothing. You are about to discover that you are everything and nothing. There is nothing to achieve because you are already all of it. There is nothing to lose because it is all you. There is no way to get it wrong because there is no "you" doing anything; it is all the actions of nature. Remember in the Bhagavad Gita where Krishna tells Arjuna that all actions arise from the three gunas or moods of nature? That's what's being described here. Arjuna

113

entered hopelessness when he found himself in the unwinnable situation of having to fight against his relatives and friends. The wisdom that came to him was to let go of the outcomes for they were not his to decide. Tamas, rajas and sattva rise and fade like the tides, causing action and inaction, war and peace. The enlightened one does not concern himself with these phenomena, knowing they are simply the moods of nature doing their thing.

Are you familiar with the second kind of hopelessness?

Perhaps it is what has brought you to this book. This book is about the divine helplessness and hopelessness that is the doorway to your enlightenment. Perhaps you are not as much of a failure as you have been thinking yourself. Perhaps you are ready for the ultimate success, the releasing of your caterpillar existence and your emergence as a being of light.

All right, let's spend a moment getting practical here. What to do when you find yourself in hopelessness. First, check that it's not just tamasic hopelessness. Make sure you've done what you can to rectify the situation. Check that you're not perhaps avoiding taking certain action because you are afraid of something. If that doesn't seem to be the case, or even if it might be, then proceed as follows:

1. Stop all efforts to feel better or to figure out what to do.

2. Go into present experience (frustration and hopelessness), feeling it directly and without reservation.

3. Expand your awareness and be receptive to Presence

4. See what wants to change.

You will recognise this as the Presence practice taught throughout this book. All you need to know is contained in the present moment when you have the courage to feel exactly what is happening and to say yes to your experience. The first step, stopping, is about letting go of the separate self who feels it has to manipulate reality and get its way. The separate self is the source of your pain, not the cure. Your fear is that hopelessness is the end of your life, but it is only the end of the separate self. When divine hopelessness appears, that is the time to celebrate!

Being positive vs. being authentic

In the new-age belief systems, especially since awareness of the Law of Attraction has become popular, it has become almost a taboo to feel anything other than constant joy, bliss, love and other positive states. The message is that if you feel grief, sadness, anger or any of those other unspiritual conditions you must buck yourself up and get positive. There is the belief that if you feel negative emotions you will attract negative circumstances into your life. While there is some truth in this, it is a partial truth. The other side of the truth is that we are human and live in duality and so will inevitably experience all the ups and downs that make up the full range of our emotional existence.

If you have tried to keep positive at all times, you will most likely have ended up feeling disappointed in yourself when you simply couldn't keep the whole love and light thing going for very long. You might have felt betrayed by your emotions and the arriving of so-called negativity into your life. You might also have come to believe that in order to be positive, you cannot afford to be authentic about the experiences that trouble you.

Or you might be reading this and saying, well it's true – I am a very positive person and I seldom feel down, and if I do I just get myself out of there. Well, I have known people like this and one thing I notice is that their refusal to feel their own sadness, anger and vulnerability borders on a phobia. The belief "I am a positive person" completely ignores the fact that no human personality can ever be fully positive because the personality is a separate identity, and this separateness means it is made of duality and will therefore always have ups and downs. "Yes, but I really do feel positive. It's just that I have this weight issue. No matter what I do I can't seem to lose all these kilograms. It's really frustrating because I have this really strict diet and I don't allow myself any sweetness at all. I just don't know why I'm putting on this weight and I'm doing so much exercise and I'm so darned positive." Can you see where the sadness has gone? Into the body. For this person, the craving for food is the only place that his inner child still has left in which to voice his fear and pain. The adult is not allowing the child's pain to be expressed, and so the child comforts himself in the only way he can – by reaching for snacks and sabotaging the tyrant adult's attempts at silencing him.

Get this – it's very important: While your negative emotions do not tell the truth about life and your current situation, they do tell the truth about your inner child's situation. Your inner child is your human side, the vulnerable, beautiful part that has been wounded and which has had to adopt defences and put on armour just to survive. Her emotions are not your enemy, they are there to be felt and embraced with compassion. "Oh no, I don't care about the past. I'm over all that stuff. I just think about love and light and then I'm fine." But is that really true, or are you just papering over the wound because you refuse to face the pain of your abandonment and your shame? Everybody is wounded – even if you had the best of childhoods. At some point you will have had to close down your light because it was not acceptable. Perhaps you were too sensitive and felt too much, or people thought you were strange and didn't seem to like you, so you had to do something, anything, to fit in. That's where the primal wounding comes in and hands you the beliefs that become part of your personality: I'm not good enough, I'm not OK as I am, I'm stupid, I'll never get it right, the world is a dangerous place, I'm a mistake, I have to do something to make it right, I have to be someone else, I don't know enough. Do you recognise yourself in there? Of course not, you're such a positive person you'd never have any of these horrible old beliefs. But just in case you do, know that you are not alone. Everyone has them unless they're enlightened. And some of the most powerful are held by those positive people who absolutely will not tolerate any negative vibes. They have denied their shadow completely, and the only place it has left to express itself is through illnesses or accidents.

I would like to propose a new definition of positivity. Positivity is not feeling positive the whole time, it is relating in a positive way to the uncomfortable feelings, thoughts and emotions that will inevitably arise in your experience. Positivity is knowing you are OK, even though you feel lousy. Positivity is having the courage to love and embrace the wounded inner child when she comes to you for comfort. Positivity is extending compassion to your fearful self and sitting with the difficult emotions as they course through your body and mind. Positivity is being willing to engage with your pain and do the inner work that restores peace. Positivity is not trying to erase clouds from the sky, it's knowing that the sun is completely unaffected by clouds, storms, tsunamis, earthquakes or whatever else is happening down here. Positivity is about being truly authentic in recognising and experiencing your thoughts, emotions and longings – no matter how apparently negative they are.

But, says the mind, if I give in to my negative feelings, maybe I'll stay there and I'll attract bad things to myself. That is one of the ego's best tricks, to convince us this is true. However, we find that when we honestly experience our anger, fear and sadness without resisting it and without buying into the story it is telling, these feelings wash over us and fade away. They are valid expressions of God, of the All, and there is nothing wrong with experiencing them. Experiencing them lets them express, and if we listen we can often catch the underlying belief that is generating them, and then real healing can happen. If we simply affirm them away all the time they'll keep coming back and we'll never get the transformation we are looking for.

Get this – negative states only activate the Law of Attraction when we buy into them and feel that they say something bad about us. It's quite possible to feel pure sadness or grief and for it not to attract bad stuff into our lives. We are simply allowing a natural expression of the All into our awareness. However, if we tell ourselves that we are bad for feeling this way, or we believe that something is happening that shouldn't, we get lost in the story, in the duality, and we are activating our disempowering beliefs about ourselves and the world. Activated negative beliefs are what attract more negativity through the Law of Attraction, not just random emotions. It is totally human to feel weak and powerless sometimes. If you can just feel this in its pure form it does not mean that you are weak and powerless, it simply means you are partaking in a common human experience. However, if you take this feeling of weakness and powerlessness and use it to trigger the belief in you that you are powerless, then you are resonating at the frequency of the victim and will open yourself to more circumstances that confirm your victimised belief about yourself.

This is actually very important to get – you aren't being positive by denying the negative, you are being truly positive when you can experience both positive and negative energies and know that you are neither. You are the space that holds both. You are truly beyond good and evil. If you buy into one of the poles at the expense of the other you activate more duality and will eventually experience the other pole. Positivity, ultimately, is knowing you are unaffected by happy or sad states, for they are just states, just objects within your unbounded awareness.

Being truly positive means having the courage to sit with your difficult emotions and extend a compassionate embrace to the part of you that is feeling hurt. Yes, that hurt part is operating on faulty information and is not awake to the natural joy, freedom and abundance of your true self, but you don't fix it by denying it and affirming it away. The hurt inner child has a message for you and a gift. The hurt and pain are pointing to a place where you have hidden your light. They are not pointing away from it, they are pointing to it. When you go into your pain, and this does not mean wallowing in it and telling poor-me stories, and truly feel the raw pain or fear, you will begin to uncover the underlying belief that is generating these states, and with loving compassion can heal them. There is good reason why you believe yourself to be less than you are. You have to honour that reason, because when you adopted it you were doing the best you could with what you knew at the time. If your parents abandoned you or you suffered some kind of abuse, the only remedy you had at the time was to side with the abuser and believe that you really were bad or faulty or unlovable. That belief helped you survive childhood, so we have to honour it. It's not something you just affirm away and get over. Well, if it's a very light belief and doesn't have much emotional charge, then sure, simply choose another belief. But some of these beliefs go all the way down to the founding moment of your personality. They are the core wounds that drive you to seek resolution and relief by achieving things in the outer world. These beliefs generate pain in the present, and this pain is actually a sacred pain because at its root is the primal wounding that has given rise to most of your experience in this life. When you face that wound, the door opens to that which has never been wounded. If you feel fundamentally unlovable because your parents didn't care for you, then facing that primal wounding brings you to the truth of who you are, which is love itself. The purpose of abuse and neglect is to awaken you to your true identity as that which is ever beyond any kind of loss. Whoever abused you took away your love, but only because you gave it to them. And you had to do it because you were a child and were innocent. You were always doing the best you could with what you knew. This means the wounding was inevitable. And because it was inevitable, there is no need to fight it or wish it didn't happen. It did happen, and it happened so you could do the work of discovering that whatever you gave away in your innocence, you still have it within you right now. True joy, love and abundance are causeless, they require no outer conditions to be met in order to be realised.

I have seen it so many times with people who come to me for this deep work, that when they finally resolve their primal woundings they discover that they – not their parents or their partners – are the ones they have been waiting for. If you were denied love as a child, you are the parent, the lover, the caregiver you have been waiting for. Nobody else has to do this work. No lover in the outer world can give you what you already have within you. All relationships will fail until you discover this. All financial plans and career schemes will fail to deliver what you truly want until you discover the wealth that is already within you. The universe is perfectly set up to awaken you. This is the Great Betrayal – the inevitability of your disillusionment whenever you try to find outside what is already inside. The world will betray you, your partners will betray you, your health will leave you, until you awaken to the Great Reversal, which is that all that you seek is within you, not outside. We have to reverse how we look at ourselves – we are not ignorant beings trying to get something from the world and make something of ourselves, we already have it all, and our work is simply to know this and then to express this in the world. You are the one you have been waiting for. Not your parents, not the world, not God, not your lovers, not your partners. You. You are the alpha and the omega. Everything you need to heal yourself is within you. As long as you keep avoiding the pain of your primal woundings you will never discover this and will always be running about in the world trying to find someone to love you or a job that pays better or a doctor that knows what's really wrong with you.

Positivity means sitting with the weeping, disappointed child within you and taking its suffering so it can be free. It is whispering the words of comfort and wisdom it needs to hear. It is facing your own abandonment and giving yourself the affirmation that you never had when you were young. Positivity is surrendering to those conditions which you cannot now change. For instance, in this moment I am surrendering to the condition of sleeplessness. For the past 8 years I've had an issue with insomnia and have had to take medication for it. Sometimes, however, it just flares up for no apparent reason and no amount of medication works. This week has been one of those times! I began this morning in fear about this insomnia and wondering how bad it would get and whether I would be left unable to function in the world. But when I sat with this experience for a while I began to notice that while tiredness and fear were part of the landscape, lightness and joy were also there. I focused on the lightness for a while, and as I did this I noticed that it expanded and began to fill me completely. Tiredness was still there, but it was barely noticeable. As I sat with this lightness and joy, curious about the play of sensations in awareness, I gently asked myself what I would love to do today. The impulse came to me to go to my computer and write something from this experience. And so I got up and began writing, and that's how this whole chapter came about. I have written it in one take, despite tiredness in the body and mind. I have found a joy and a compassion in me. I am the rest I so desire. I surrender to this condition of sleeplessness, knowing I am doing what is in my power to do. I notice the fear that still arises when I think of it but I do nothing – neither trying to get rid of it nor buying into more of its story. I am compassionate with myself, giving myself the care that I need. I am open to guidance about what can be done to bring healing. I am feeling my way into a sense of peace about this. I notice some strength arise, a knowing that whatever happens I will be all right. This is positivity.

The use and abuse of affirmations

A big part of the positive thought movement is the use of affirmations. Affirmations are phrases or statements that express a desired emotion or positive outcome. I have seen affirmations being used to great effect, but I have also seen them being used in a way that has unintended negative consequences. Essentially, if we are using affirmations as a way of keeping everything all sunny and shiny and if we are hoping to attract only good things into our lives, we are buying into the very duality we are trying to avoid. It's simply not possible to have everything going right for us all the time, and trying to manipulate reality to bring us only nice, shiny stuff is a dream of the ego. Spirit wants one thing for you, and that is for you to awaken to your identity as that which is beyond good and evil. If you keep banishing evil you will keep seeing evil and the light that you long for will always be out of your reach.

If affirmations are being used to avoid the deeper work that wants to happen then they will not lead to your intended outcome. For example, if a bad feeling arises and it comes from a past hurt that is wanting to be healed, then frantically reciting positive affirmations will not serve your highest good. It will take you out of the healing and create a positive effect that has very little depth and resilience. It might help you in the short-term, but it is not very likely to provide the change you are really seeking. You will know if you are doing this by the feeling of urgency that drives your affirmations – it's like you are desperately trying to stay ahead of a demon that is chasing you, and if you stop for just a minute you're going to be overwhelmed.

So does this mean you throw out affirmations altogether?

No, it means that you use affirmations not to escape the darker emotions but to awaken the positive energy that is already within you.

For instance, suppose you are worrying about your work situation. Perhaps you are out of work or your workflow has run dry, so now you are feeling anxious about this. First, simply feel the anxiety and be with it for a while. Inquire into the underlying beliefs that support this anxiety. For example, you might realise you are falling into the belief that scarcity is real or that you are not worthy of success. This is the deeper healing that your anxiety is directing you to look at. So spend some time breathing into that pain and just noticing the beliefs that no longer serve you. They probably won't just disappear in a flash, but at least now you know that the source of the anxiety is not the lack of work, it's that you believe in lack itself or that you are somehow lacking in yourself.

Now, with this realisation, you are ready to start feeling better. From here you can feel your way into positive affirmations that build upon the truth that is already within you. And notice I say "feel your way" because if you just apply some standard affirmation you are again trying to jump into somebody else's idea of who you should be. Feeling into it means you connect with your belief in lack and you ask what is a more beneficial belief. The best affirmations are those that arise within you as expressions of pre-existing truth. In this example, you might realise, "Hey, I actually am worthy and creative and I can find work." Then your affirmation might be, "Rewarding work is flowing into my life, I am seeing opportunities all around me and I am grateful for everything I already have."

Now this affirmation speaks back to the truth from which it sprang and evokes more of it. So your inner being, hearing you speak the words of the affirmation, gets affirmed in its knowing and offers you more of the same. In a short while you will be feeling good in a very authentic way and will be resonating at the frequency of possibility.

Do you see how this approach gets to the positive by first being authentic with the negative? Start seeing the negative as simply an indicator of where compassionate awareness wants to flow. There is something of great value for you in the dark. Only by going into it does it release and set you free. The method is first to engage with the dark and then to find the turning point, which is often an insight into the underlying belief that is causing the pain. Only once the turning point is reached are you ready to affirm the positive and bring more of it into your life.

Another way you can look at this is to imagine a surfer waiting out in the ocean for a wave. Does she lie there affirming a wave into existence if there are none at the moment? No. What she does is she waits until a wave begins to build, and then she rides with it. Your affirmations are like surfboards – they are not there for creating waves of positive energy, they are there for riding the waves as they arise. To catch a wave, you sometimes have to wait in the empty ocean doing nothing at all but simply being alive and present, surrendering to the moment as it is. When the ocean is ready to shape itself into a wave, you will be ready to catch it.

Having said that, there are times when you really just need to get positive quickly. For example, if you're about to get up on stage and deliver a speech and you're having a panic attack, now might not be the right time to inquire into limiting beliefs. If you need a quick fix, then I recommend the HeartMath coherence techniques. This is not to say that HeartMath is a quick fix, but it can be used that way if needed.

Does the Now tolerate only good feelings?

Another reason to leave thoughts and feelings alone is that in the moment they appear, they are part of the Now and are fully accepted by Life. This includes your unhappiness, sadness and despair. It includes the not-nice things you do when you feel threatened or when your needs are not being met. If you take away all the stories of how you *should* feel and just stay with how you *do* feel, then you will realise that the Now has no judgement about your feelings and actions. When you allow it all you become one with it and the little self, the ego, is at rest. You could say that in your moment of oneness with your discomfort you, as separate being, disappear and only Life remains, appearing as this separate form with your name. However, when you believe you shouldn't feel this way you separate yourself from what is and create a duality. Now ego is in charge again. Ironically, by trying to do good you have increased the separation that keeps you forever locked out of the Good. Ultimately, even the appearance of ego is simply an appearance of the Now, so there is nothing to fight against. The point is that when you get into shoulds and shouldn'ts you are arguing with reality and putting a conceptual ideal out there. A concept is a dream within a dream – it takes you out of now and puts you on the never ending road to Shangri-la or La-la land, or whatever heaven you hope is waiting for you.

All right, so I've had my rant against trying to change thoughts and manipulate reality, now what's the alternative?

The alternative is that you simply feel what you are feeling with the understanding that you are feeling a thought, and no thought is real. All thoughts are abstractions, made-up stories, and they never touch reality. If you try to change thoughts and feelings to something better, you are simply affirming the illusory thinker, and the root of your suffering will remain. You are trying to turn an iron cage into a golden cage. And yes, a golden cage is nicer, especially if it has an ocean view, but is that really what you are looking for?

If you leave all your tampering and fixing and manipulating alone and simply allow current experience, you might become aware of a deeper presence beneath the thoughts and feelings. This is the realm of causeless joy. It is only perceived when you let go of causes and conditions and welcome yourself exactly as you are. This, as you are, is reality. There is no greater or lesser reality. This is it. You are it. You are the divine unfolding of causeless joy. And yes, that includes your faults, your failures and your endless seeking. Right now, simply receive yourself as you are. You are good enough. Nothing needs to be added or taken away. Cease at last with the endless addition and subtraction of the self and be in the place where nothing is weighed and judged. The one who reads these words is God. There is no-one else.

Before continuing, let's spend a few more moments here in this space of receiving and accepting. What you are seeking is not on the next page, it is here right now. Take a slow, appreciative breath and receive yourself exactly as you are. Receive your pain, your failure, your joy, your sadness. Receive your vulnerable humanity. You cannot get it right, you cannot fix everything. Let it all go and simply sit here a while and feel how it is to be you right now. Up or down, happy or sad, the light of awareness shines equally on all. Receive yourself with compassion and mercy. Do not chase away the wounded child within who cries for love and understanding. Do not banish yourself for your imagined sins. Receive the wounded one, the misunderstood one. Receive him. Receive her. Be the parent she never had, the friend she always longed for. You are the one. Yes, you.

The hidden power of longing

Under the model of Materialism, the things we desire and long for indicate things in our lives that are missing. If we long for wealth, we set about trying to get money to fill the sense that right now we are poor. In this understanding, desires and longings are a source of energy to do things, but they also become a source of pain. When we assume that we do not have what we long for, we are denying the truth of our completeness and will feel the pain of exile from Being.

From the understanding of Emergence, however, longings are seen as indicators of what we are already. A longing is a creative tension between emptiness and fullness, between that which seems to be missing and the truth of its unrecognised presence. When you first become aware of a longing there is sometimes a reaction away from it because it feels like an unmet need, which is painful. You are seeing the pure absence side of it. If you are feeling lonely, for example, you will not want to experience more of the longing for companionship because this only seems to evoke a sense of loss or lack. However, the beauty of longings is that while they seem to tell us about an absence, they actually arise from the presence of that which we seek. If we did not have love within us, we could not long for love and partnership. It is love that is calling, but in our innocence we assume that it is calling from out there somewhere, wherever love abides, and that we have to do something to get it. We feel certain that the pain of this lack of love means love is not within us. We say we have a need for love. We long for something we do not have. So we try to medicate this need away through alcohol, drugs, sex, work or whatever activity seems to numb the pain.

Another favourite drug is endless seeking. We are continually seeking more money, better partners, a perfect present moment. We are seeking the end of our discomfort, the arrival of something else that is not this. Some of us end up seeking God. We are trying to ease the pain of a need, but we are looking in the wrong place. Because we feel lacking we assume that what we seek is over there, outside of us. When we interpret this lack as a need, we suffer. But when we begin to feel it as a longing, we begin to awaken to its beauty, which is that it is calling to us from within.

In the Christian mystic tradition, Christ is said to answer the anguished seeker with the words, "Console yourself, you would not seek me unless you had already found me." In the end it is God who is praying to God. It is God who seeks the love that it already is, in this way discovering itself and becoming conscious of what it is. This is all happening as you, right now. Is it love you seek, or wealth, or approval, or enlightenment, or health, or the parents you never had? From duality consciousness there is some other person or state that contains the salvation you are looking for, but from union, from the condition of not-two, there is only you, now and ever. The longing is your desire to know yourself. It is Life's desire to know itself. But first it must hide itself and pretend that it has lost what it can never lose. And so we set out into the world to find the holy balm or the medicine or the lover that will restore us, and yet what a hopeless quest! To find rest we can do only one thing ... sit with the longing, entertain it as a troublesome guest, and let it guide us to the source.

But here is why we do not easily do that: Before we can find the positive side of the longing we sometimes encounter the hole, the void, the primal wounding that caused us to lose sight of what we had. It appears as an emptiness, a discomfort. The more we simply sit with the longing and notice it, the closer we get to the moment that longing was created. The mind wants to keep us away and tells us all sorts of alarming stories about what will happen if we carry on down this road. We will go mad, we will be bored, we will have to face the void, we will lose everything, we will die. The approach to the God-self, or Being, can evoke the fear of death, the fear of annihilation, because the ego-self cannot imagine its survival in a world without boundaries. It will tell you how terrible this is going to be and that you should turn back now or become a zombie, but you go on. You encounter your loss, your emptiness. And guess what ... you do not disappear in a puff of smoke! You are still here. The mind is quiet, it has not died after all – only the idea of yourself has died, and only for this moment. You experience clarity, curiosity, aliveness, love, joy. Now you are awake to your true nature, and you see why this is such an open secret. Nobody tells you that you have to go through the pain of loss of self in order to gain your Self. They tell you to affirm away the pain and stay positive at all costs. But this is a deeper kind of positivity, the kind that knows you are well no matter what emotional state appears in your awareness.

This message is for those who are tired of trying to feel OK and to get it right; it is for those who have been seeking and who still have not found. So let us give up the search, just for now. Let us find what is here, in this humble, messy moment. Notice the simple fact of your existence as you hold this book, taking in these words. While you were so absorbed in reading, reading was happening all by itself. Reading was happening effortlessly, without you doing anything. For this moment, lose track of the meaning of these words and notice the presence that absorbs these words. Is there any separation between this presence and these words and the hand that holds this book? There is no distance. These words are you. Throw away the meaning, throw away your assumptions about who has written this and who is reading, and stay with this moment, this still, precious moment in which this act of reading is unfolding. There is no doer here, there is just the reading. Feel the animal existence of this moment, the language-less original innocence of this unfolding. There is no you or I here, there is no author or reader, these words have never appeared anywhere in the world until now. Feel that. The appearance of words, the appearance of meaning, their disappearance.

Just turn on the light!

If a child is scared of her dark room because of the monsters, do you tell her to do battle with the monsters? Do you tell her she needs to face her demons and overcome her fear? Or do you flick the light switch so she can see there are no monsters in the room? When you are in the light, what seemed a problem before is no longer a problem. There are no monsters, only the endarkened thinking that makes us think there are. The question of whether you should fix your issues and defeat your monsters no longer applies when you switch on the light. Switching on the light in your own life means looking at your current situation and seeing that what you take to be a monster is simply your own thinking. Your mind will tell you that as a spiritual being or as a psychologically mature person you should work on your stuff, and the implication of this is that if you are not yet happy or completely well rounded you have work to do. When you have work to do, you are saying that you are not there yet. Not yet. Always almost there, and never actually here. But what if we switched on the light and saw this exact situation bathed in the light of non-judgemental, non-personal consciousness where it simply would not occur to one to apply a label to one's experience? You would simply notice this present arising, this unfolding

Now. In it, things happen. If you apply no language to divide it up, can you claim ownership of the choices and actions you seem to be participating in, or is it just a flow of appearance?

Turning on the light means seeing that this as it is, exactly as it is, is where it's meant to be. This is where flow has brought you. Your approval or disapproval of the situation is also part of that same flow. Take one step back and notice how things happen and then mental comments happen. If you feel lack or stress of any kind, take one step back and observe the appearance of the lack or stress in your awareness. In other words, take your attention off the apparent cause of the lack and place it on the appearance of it in your awareness. This is the key practice. Nothing is causing your feeling of lack other than an interpretation of neutral existence. And yet this very misinterpretation, once made, is itself part of the flow and is inseparable from it. If you berate yourself for having fallen into illusion, take one step back and notice that your beating yourself up is one more appearance in a play of appearances. Once you see this, do you still need to beat yourself up?

Who is choosing? The small self, the ego, is apparently free to choose. And whatever it chooses is accepted without question by the greater Will, thus becoming part of the flow of all life. When you see that you have been interpreting from the limited perspective of small self, you no longer need to continue interpreting in this way. When you feel lack and stress, simply stop, notice and allow. The allowing brings you to the deeper wisdom that even your ignorance and resistance is part of what is, and there is nothing that needs to change. Everything that appears has already been accepted by Life itself, and you are not separate from that life. Yet when you see this and fully embrace the pain or lack of the moment without needing to change it, change is free to happen. The release happens not by avoiding the difficult present by trying to think positive but by experiencing it fully and discovering the flow that has already embraced your resistance. The light is switched on and the problem is no longer a problem, simply a circumstance.

"I'm not making it"

A friend of mine was counting up her month's income and the thought came, "I'm not making it." It was a familiar thought, one that had troubled her for years as she tried to get her various businesses profitable. Before, this thought had triggered feelings of shame and anxiety. But this time the thought came and it didn't bite. Or rather, there was a small gap in which she knew she had the choice to believe in the thought or not. The temptation was there, because objectively she was not making it financially. But now in one instant of liberation she noticed the thought surfacing in her awareness and she saw that she didn't have to get on board and ride it. The thought merely described a circumstance, it did not relate to her personally. She wasn't making it, but her "I" was no longer involved in the thought. This is the essence of what we are describing in this book. No matter what your circumstances, there is a doorway to freedom right in the midst of it all.

Doing this work increases the space between a thought and your ownership of it and your believing in it. You do not have to own or believe any thought, especially any one that tells you that you are not already here, not already fully worthy. Even your unworthiness is part of the flow of God. Once you know this, all worthiness is restored. Your true worth contains worthiness and unworthiness, making it and not making it. There is nothing outside this appearance, this very now, this hand moving to write, there is no author here and no reader, only this divine enactment. How glorious, how luminous. This love I feel as I write, knowing there is nothing beyond this moment, there is no I who writes and no reader who awaits. This divine play, taking shape through me, as me, as this apparent separate being apparently doing something. Right now, in this moment, notice how effortlessly these words appear for you, how reading is happening. How do you know there is any author who was here before you? Right now there is only this appearing, this tender, luminous, ordinary miracle of the appearance of reading. My friend, is this not a miracle? Here is the presence of God, here, in these ordinary words, this ordinary moment, nothing added, nothing removed, all your circumstances exactly as they are. Can you let them go for now and just be here, as this untouched light that by some incredible mystery is taking shape as you. How did you know how to write these words? What a mystery! There is nothing outside of the moment in which you read this line. This is it!

7. FINAL WORDS

You gotta have faith!

People are fond of saying, "I'll believe it when I see it." Even if they don't consciously say this, underneath they are still largely basing their perceptions of themselves on the evidence they find in the world. If we don't have much money, we believe we are poor. If we don't have a loving partner, we believe we have a scarcity of love. We are allowing the outer conditions to say something about our identity – and that's a recipe for suffering.

The inside-out model offers freedom from the imprisoning effects of judgement based on outer conditions. But there's one obstacle that stops most of us: to really work the inside-out perspective you've got to be up for the challenge of accessing your inner state of having and fullness before evidence of this fullness shows up in the world. The real truth is: "You will see it when you believe it."

If you don't have much money, you've got to access your inner feelings of wellbeing and abundance and really *feel* wealthy. To most people, that will seem impossible. And yet, if you have been following the processes in this book, you will know what to do. The moment you feel poor or lacking in any way, simply stop, experience that feeling fully, and become aware of what else you notice. What surrounds the experience of being poor? What is the ground in which that feeling arises? That ground is your ever-present, abundant, always-worthy Self.

For instance, a moment ago I was having another one of those panic moments about my work and how to get clients. The inner critic came up and told me I shouldn't be wasting my time writing a book – I should rather be out there doing "real" work. So, recognising that I was suffering from perceptions rather than reality, I spent a few moments observing the discomfort and listening to the voices giving me dire predictions of my future. I began to notice that despite all this noise going on, I was also in touch with a deep stillness and sense of wellbeing. I posed a question in this stillness: What do I need to do to get a flow of abundance in my life?

Immediately the answer came back: "But I am already so abundant!"

Then I knew that it was true. But for the conditions I was imposing on my abundance, I had everything I needed. Right in that moment, all was good. I really felt the goodness of that moment and I knew that I needed no outer state of wealth to confirm my inner state. The outer state will take care of itself. My work is to connect with the inner state which is always true, without exception. It is wealth and abundance that is writing this book. It is my desire to share what I know and to offer something of value to the world. And it is my great mission to support myself and others in ending the suffering caused by judging ourselves based on the evidence of our lives. Our true nature is causeless. It is always and ever worthy, no matter what is happening in our lives. You do not need to change or improve anything to discover your freedom. Your wealth, love, success and happiness are already here. Do not wait for them to show up in your world before you believe them. You have to believe them first. This is the meaning of faith. Not faith in another person, teacher or ideology, but faith that despite appearances, you are good, worthy, abundant and a perfect expression of the One.

Remember the Great Betrayal? The world will eventually betray your efforts to arrange things to give you positive feelings about yourself. If circumstances are currently betraying you, then that's great news! It means you are ready to find the source of wellbeing and abundance within you. Be of courage as you go through the withdrawal symptoms of removing your attention from so-called evidence in the world and finding it in the wealth of your own being. It can be a bit of a walk through darkness. In the darkness you will have a choice to go into despair or into enlightenment. Which do you choose today?

The path of compassion and courage

Living from the inside-out understanding brings effortlessness into your life – but I would be lying if I told you that maintaining and deepening this perspective was easy. Some of us are lucky enough to have sudden awakening experiences, but for most of us, well, we're taking the scenic route. We get to face our fears and uproot our outdated beliefs one by one. We get to discover the value of compassion for ourselves as we embark on a journey that can sometimes feel lonely and a bit scary.

The fact is, you are going up against a society and a world that has very little understanding of this view. On top of that, you will have grown up in the outside-in way and will have absorbed its tenets in the same way you picked up language and all those other things that have become an unconscious part of your personality. It's like we are hardwired to search outside ourselves for answers rather than to trust the stillness of Being. So making the turnaround is not usually just a matter of deciding that from henceforth you are going to see things differently. That's a great start, but when challenges come, you will probably run back to the safety of the old ways. That is why all spiritual traditions that teach the inside-out understanding place great emphasis on having a teacher and being part of a community of support. They recognise that to really ground the inside-out approach requires practice, tenacity, great courage, and reminders from fellow pilgrims when you inevitably lose your way.

I have my own such support network in the Zen Coaching school I am part of. I know that support from a fellow coach is just a phone call away. The real benefit of having a coaching partner is that your partner is able to model a state of coherence and Being while you go through your experience of disconnection from Being. To have someone on the other end of the phone who listens attentively without buying into your story or challenging you or doing anything to shift you to where they think you should go is revelatory. Without doing anything except maintaining connection with their own being, they enable you to rediscover that frequency within you. The difficulty you were experiencing is absorbed into the greater Self and you are no longer at odds with it.

So having a supportive partner is invaluable in living this understanding. If you don't have one, that's also OK. With or without a partner, the real transformation comes in actually living the teachings. Here's what you do:

1. Make it your highest priority to tune in to the state of noticing as often as you can. While working, while washing dishes, before sleeping, on waking ... become aware of your own existence as the noticing space that contains all objects of awareness. At first this might make you feel uncomfortable, but it does get easier.

2. Meet all challenges, low moods and afflictive states with an attitude of compassionate and courageous observation.

Stop trying to fix them and simply find the yes in present experience. If pain is here, feel it completely. If anger is here, let it well up. Make space for all appearances, avoiding none and attaching to none.

3. As you go about your daily life, tune in to the presence that is beyond all occurrences. Even if pain, anger or other states are present, notice what is noticing them. See if you can become aware of the already-existing flavours of Being as your stories come to rest and you dwell in that which is ever beyond story.

4. If you need to make decisions or take action, make sure you are rooted in Being and essence before doing so. Surrender to your inner nature, and allow it to decide for you. The core understanding of the inside-out model is that you don't have to do all the work yourself. Being, God, Universe, the implicate order does the work.

The main qualities you will need to bring to this are compassion and courage: compassion for the human part of you that will inevitably suffer in this world of duality, and courage to stand your ground as your old instincts try to pull you into dramas of winning and losing. You will inevitably be thrown off course and be challenged by people and by life. You will think you are a fool for walking this path, but when you try to go back to the old way you find that that door is closed to you. You can't un-know what you know. The only way forward is onward into the not-knowing of divine will.

You are actively surrendering to the life that lives through you and as you. Let your fear about this and that feeling of emptiness and groundlessness that inevitably arises be just one more object in awareness. Even groundlessness has a ground. You are that ground of Being. You are nothing that happens. You are no possession. You are nothing that can be named. You are not even the one reading this. Reading is happening.

Herein lies your mind's greatest fear and also your greatest freedom. You are not you ... and yet here you are! Is that not a miracle worth celebrating?

Beyond happiness

It's often said that happiness is a choice. And it is ... to a point. Sometimes, too much choosing of happiness can be an avoidance of pain and the shadow aspects that want to be felt and experienced. A general rule of thumb is this: when unhappy, choose to be happy; and if that doesn't work, surrender to the unhappy sensation and experience it completely. Let there be no separation between you and unhappiness, pain, sadness or whatever other imp of Beelzebub is feasting on your innards. Let the struggle cease. In releasing the struggle you find the Now, the place of deep allowing. The pain will still be there, but there is peace around it. Spirit is merely curious about pain, it has no judgement of it.

If you are suffering some kind of mental, emotional or physical pain, perhaps you would like to spend a few moments in surrender to it now. Let it take you over completely. Your resistance is futile, haven't you noticed? We are not required to deny our humanity in order to be enlightened. Our humanity is our physical and psychological presence in the world. It is unavoidably part of duality and the play of light and dark. It is Christ on the cross. Accidents will happen. Old age and illness will catch up with all of us. Our humanity is vulnerable; it does not escape the crucifixion.

Happiness is a choice to look on the bright side of whatever shows up, but it also needs to go deeper to those times when we can find no bright side whatsoever. I have written this book from both my bright side and my dark side. I have not told you about all the times I lay in bed too full of fear to get out and face the day. I have not told you about the demons who sit at my shoulder and tell me I am a fraud for writing a book about joy when I spend so much time in their dark domain. Though in the end, who better? We teach what we most need to learn. This book is an elaborate note-to-self, a reminder for when I fall off the wagon and can no longer see the light. I am confessing this so that I do not inadvertently set you up for self-criticism when you inevitably find yourself on your own cross of trial and doubt. I feel safe to confide in you now, for the terminally happy people would all have abandoned this book by page 5. It is only us here, the last-gaspers and desperados, the ragged pilgrims, neglected prophets, god-drunk lovers and sainted whores. Which one are you?

We are the ones who have journeyed beyond happiness. What have we discovered? That the light does not judge. It does not even judge the judging that inevitably happens. We have discovered the willingness to sit with ourselves in a field of compassion when our pain is triggered and the unhealed parts of our souls come forward to be recognised. I believe that many who are reading this will be undergoing that great healing work we call the Dark Night of the Soul. From the outside, it looks like you're not making it. Things are falling apart. In this time it is easy to compare yourself with others and wonder why you are failing so magnificently while they are striding ahead. Once upon a time you thought you'd really gotten a hold on this thing called life, and now it's all gone south. Well, could it be that now is the time when you are finally ready to exercise the depth of compassion required to heal the old wounds that come from before you can even remember? In these times it is difficult to just be happy. No matter how much you choose happiness, only grief seems to arise. A few seconds of happiness does little more than invite more trouble in. I am writing this so that you might cease to chastise yourself for your failure in the happiness race.

Happiness might not be for you right now, but joy is. Joy is knowing you are the light, even when you can see no trace of it. The sun is ignorant of its own luminescence. Only that which is not the sun can see the sun. When God disappears from your life, do not assume it is gone. Perhaps it is because you have fallen into it and are one with it. We have so many fantasies about what oneness should feel like, but really it is oneness with everything that arises, both the light and the dark.

The Indian sage J. Krishnamurti was once asked his secret to happiness. In a soft voice, he said to the audience, "My secret is this: I don't mind what happens."

He was pointing to the choicelessness of life, to the fact that things happen and we are not as in control as we think we are. Light happens, dark happens. To arrive at this awareness requires an apparent choice in the moment – a choice to stand your ground in the face of all temptation to go back into your life and try to fix things. You choose between the promise of conditional happiness or the eternal truth of your nature. You are already the love and wealth you seek, and until you carry this knowing with you in all moments you might need to choose to discover it in those moments when it appears to be absent. You are joy, regardless of how you feel.

To make this choice you might have to become intimately acquainted with failure. Any form of happiness that is conditional on certain people being in your life and on certain living standards being met and on any ideal being upheld – even the most spiritual – is bound to be exposed for what it is, an interesting diversion into the world of form. Failure, it turns out, is your best friend. It is the meteor that arrives in your life with a cleansing fire to burn out the world of illusion and open you to that which you could never imagine. Surrender to that over which you have no control. Life is living you, have you noticed? Where there is control there is separation. But you have been chosen to discover unity in this lifetime. Yes, you.

Entering Presence

And now it looks like we are coming to the end of this exploration, so let's just spend some time in the awareness of our true nature.

As you are reading this, perhaps you would like to slow down and appreciate the ordinary miracle of your breath, of this consciousness that is always simply here, now. You are not lacking anything, no matter what circumstances seem to be telling you. If you have breath, if you have awareness, then God is fully present in and as you. This is so obvious we miss it in all our seeking after something better. We think God or life or some other authority wants us to get it right and to grow and to overcome our weaknesses; we imagine there is some accounting going on somewhere and we are always a few pennies short of what we owe. Well, my friend, we can go on searching for those pennies forever and we will never find them, because in this world of appearances there will always be something missing and life will always be unsatisfactory. We might find rest and pleasure in moments, and then the basic missingness of life reasserts itself, and away we go, looking for that magical substance that will fill the void.

Are you not already tired of the search? Are you not ready to abandon yourself into the brokenness of your human self and discover that this too is God. Nothing is missing, there is only an appearance of missing. The appearance of loss is a pointer to that which is ever beyond loss.

There's a reason you're not getting it right, and it's because you can never get it right and you're not supposed to. If you got everything right you'd think you were doing it and that you'd mastered life. You'd become a minor god with an ego as big as the sun. That is why you can't succeed. It is Mercy that time and again rescues you from the illusion of your personhood. You are meant to fail because the little self that fails is mortal and is meant to break open so that the unnameable Self might be revealed. This is the one you have been longing for and running away from your whole life. This is the one who sends its agents to trip you up so you might know that where you are going is not the place you truly long to be. Life wants to recognise itself in all things, not just in one little thing called you. We are all going to die, have you noticed? There is no escaping sickness and mishap. The crucifixion is not to be escaped for it is the very doorway of escape. In suffering all, in being most human, you discover that which is most divine. Compassion is not interested in your shiny life and your mansion by the sea, it wants to know if it can love everything. Again and again it places itself in the mud and asks, Can I love even this? Heartbreak is the theme song of love. Everything will leave you, all promises will be unmade. You might pray for this cup to pass you by but the light has no interest in your preservation, it is interested only in whether it can recognise itself in all that appears. Forgive them, for they know not what they do. Though they crucify you, you see within their hearts and find only innocence. This is the mastery you seek.

Therefore if you are in pain now and if there is something that feels like it should not be happening and that you are powerless and don't know what to do next, consider that love has sent its agents to awaken you to that which is ever beyond your circumstances. Right now, if you are suffering, let go for a moment with all your fixing and simply be here. Breathe. Offer praise for the simple miracle of being alive. Notice how perfectly you are supported on the chair or on the earth or wherever you are. God, Life, is not asking you to get it right, it is asking you to notice what is already right. It does not recognise loss as something that needs to be fixed. Does the earth cry when winter comes? Some day you will also be gone, but right now the fire is burning. Do you not feel the fire of pure Being in your heart? Look deeper, underneath the hurt, to that raging stillness, the ecstasy of causeless existence. What is this awareness that reads these words? Is this not the miracle you seek? I write this from my own pain and from all that resists my intentions. Pain is the one that has come to awaken me to your presence. Without my suffering I would not have known of your burdens. Pick up your cross, friend, and be of good cheer. You are in the right place for the transformation you have been praying for. Surrender, surrender. This cup will not pass you by until its work is done. With great love, from my mortal self to yours.

RESOURCES

It's a very rare person who awakens to their true nature all on their own. Most of us need the guidance of teachings and the support of wise friends. So here are some resources that you might find supportive:

Personal coaching from the author

Firstly, you are welcome to contact me with questions or for coaching from the perspective of Being. In this coaching you will get to discover the peace and joy of your true nature, no matter what is happening in your life. The recognition of fulfilment, ease and wisdom as the essence of all your experience will free you from negative judgements of yourself and your circumstances, releasing great resources of energy and creativity in your life. I sincerely look forward to working with you.

Contact me through my website: **www.russelbrownlee.com** or **www.facebook.com/CauselessJoy**.

Learn Zen Coaching

Some of the core insights that led me to write this book were gained through my contact with Kåre Landfald and his school of Zen Coaching. The intention of Zen Coaching is to support people in recognizing and living their true nature as free, spacious awareness. If you are looking for a very accessible course of learning and practical inquiry with a supportive network of friends, this is the place: **www.zen-coaching.com**

The Emergence model

For more on the Emergence model, see Derek Rydall:
www.derekrydall.com

And most of all, consult your own Self in the stillness
of Being.

www.russelbrownlee.com

www.ingramcontent.com/pod-product-compliance
Lightning Source LLC
Chambersburg PA
CBHW020544030426
42337CB00013B/978